GIVE ME SHELTER

ARCHITECTURE TAKES ON THE HOMELESS CRISIS

Edited by Sofia Borges / R. Scott Mitchell
Forward by Mayor Eric Garcetti

MADWORKSHOP

ORO
EDITIONS

CONTENTS

"We cannot accept homelessness as the new normal."

People in every corner of Los Angeles understand that homelessness is the moral crisis of our time. There is no other aspect of our daily lives that so thoroughly exposes the devastating consequences of poverty and inequality. We all feel compassion for neighbors who are huddled on sidewalks, unable to escape the cold rain. It fills us all with outrage to know that mothers and fathers — many of whom have worn this country's uniform — are left begging at freeway exits. Everyone's heart breaks knowing that an entire generation of Angelenos have grown up to believe that streets and alleys lined with tents are a normal part of their city's landscape.

No more. We cannot accept homelessness as the new normal. We're not here to address, manage, or reduce it—we're here to end homelessness once and for all. That's why I created LA's first Office of Economic Opportunity, so that City Hall could put a tighter focus on the needs of the most vulnerable by making housing more affordable and accessible. Angelenos are joining this urgent work: in the last year, voters approved historic local investments—billions of dollars to get people into homes and connect them with the services they need to stay off the streets.

We must work together to deliver historic change. The designs in *Give Me Shelter*—which map out transitional communities where Angelenos can live in safety and privacy while we build more permanent supportive housing—reflect that unity of purpose. All of the contributors to this book deserve our gratitude and admiration. Their work reflects the very spirit of Los Angeles: a city in which people not only believe in a better future, but a city in which we all work to manifest that better future for everyone.

Eric Garcetti
Mayor of Los Angeles

I take homelessness personally.

While I am relatively new to working on this topic, I am not new to the topic itself. Three years ago today, my brother Daren passed away as a result of his struggles with homelessness and schizophrenia. Treated and criminalized as a second class citizen for most of his life, he died a preventable death after being denied his right to medical care. His death coincided with my return to Los Angeles after several years abroad. In my absence, my hometown had become unaffordable and cast a new legion of people out on the streets. Many of us, more than we'd like to admit, are just a pay check or two away from being homeless ourselves. Shelter should be a human right, not a luxury reserved for those who can afford it.

My grief over my personal loss was amplified by all the suffering I saw. My professional work no longer mattered to me. I was not making a difference. I wanted to start, but didn't know how. I paced at the edge of the issue for several months in search of an opening. I began to observe the people experiencing homelessness in my neighborhood and photographed them from afar. I didn't talk to them. I wasn't ready yet. Instead I looked at what they had with them—a certain colorful blanket, a puppy calendar, a broom, a bouquet of flowers. I took these photos home and began to house each person in my imagination. I drew quaint A-frames and modernist Case-Study houses over them. I took a person sleeping on a bus stop bench and transported them into their very own protected living room. I changed an older gentleman walking down the street with no place to go into a scene of him exploring the topiary gardens in front of his classical villa. With each overlay, I asked the question: if these people weren't here, where would they be? By changing their context, could I change how we saw them? I exhibited this series at the USC School of Architecture. This would be my first time publicly acknowledging the homelessness in my own family but also my first professional call to arms about the issue. To my surprise, the school welcomed my candor and paired me with R. Scott Mitchell—now one of my closest friends and allies—to co-teach the MADWORKSHOP Homeless Studio. This class would focus on the underserved and highly stigmatized area of emergency stabilization housing, also known as "bridge housing."

This course would be my own personal bootcamp into the scope and complexity of the LA homeless crisis. I used the chance to call up my heroes and learn. We flew in Betty Chinn from Humboldt County and picked her brain about her container housing project for the homeless in Eureka. "They don't think like you do," she chided after reviewing our first designs. We revised accordingly. We invited the outspoken legend Ted Hayes, the mastermind behind Dome Village—the longest

Photo Credit: John Cizmas

standing homeless community in Los Angeles—to critique our students' schematic layouts. We consulted with Michael Maltzan and Skid Row Housing Trust, the Midnight Mission, The People Concern (LAMP), and Downtown Women's Center to learn about what works and what doesn't when transitioning people back into housing and how design can assist in that process.

When Scott and I developed this class we decided that none of our efforts could be speculative. Too much was and still is at stake for another hypothetical exercise. Could design help us get people housed sooner? We intended to find out. We embarked on a number of efforts, some more successful than others. We wanted to try a little bit of everything and see what worked best. Our end goal was to give the embattled typology of the homeless shelter an extreme, city-supported makeover. We intended to argue that a shelter didn't have to be large, or ugly, or even permanent.

The first task we gave to our students focused on establishing compassion. We studied homelessness as an architectural typology and the homeless themselves as master builders. We looked at their existing structures and techniques and found ways to streamline and improve upon them. The class created a series of nomadic shelters that introduced simple moves for security and comfort. Some students modified shopping carts so you could actually lock your belongings. Others built bicycle caravans that elevated you off of the ground when you slept. The exercise tackled issues of threshold, camouflage, mobility, and community. This was a quick and informal solution, not an end goal.

Next, we brought down the tiny house artist Gregory Kloehn from Oakland to do a one week workshop with the students. They had two days to scavenge Los An-

geles for trash. They returned to school with their new-found treasures and turned the main courtyard into an enormous garbage pile. USC spent the next five days watching us transform this trash heap into three tiny homes for the homeless. Some of the whimsical design details included a roof made out of a skewed camper top and a repurposed refrigerator door that doubled as an emergency exit. The workshop underscored our belief that everything and everyone deserves a second chance. Greg moved the homes to an encampment in Vernon and gave Marvin, Guillermo, and Gio a key to each. I spent the next several Saturdays visiting the new residents of the homes, learning their stories, and watching them grow comfortable in their spaces. Marvin told me he finally felt safe. I felt like I had solved homelessness and absolved myself all in one action. Then the City came for the encampment and our tiny homes. I was devastated. As time passed, I realized that the City wasn't wrong in their actions. This wasn't a solution, this was an informal bandaid, albeit one I had gotten very attached to. This setback led to our current alliance with the City of Los Angeles and the final project of the course—Homes for Hope.

Homes for Hope gave the students the opportunity to work with a real client, on a real site, for a real project. We partnered with Ken Craft, the CEO of Hope of the Valley Rescue Mission. Scott and I didn't know how far we would get, but our students, client, and partners at the city soon exceeded our expectations. What began as a simple desire for change quickly evolved into a real solution.

It is cheaper to house our homeless than to continue to do nothing. And yet, an incredible barrier exists in our ability to conceive a solution that works as a city. But we've got to. We can't afford to wring our hands anymore. The Not In My Back Yard (NIMBY) argument no longer holds up. Homelessness in Los Angeles has increased 23% since 2016. This epidemic has already reached your back yard. We cannot wait two to five years to get people off the streets. We've got to do these things, as imperfect as they may be. Moving forward as a society is always a work in progress. Here is our draft. We look forward to your revision.

Sofia Borges
Director of MADWORKSHOP
Lecturer at USC School of Architecture

I have driven down Ohio Avenue as it runs below the 405 Freeway more times than I can count. Over the past year, I have watched the number of homeless encampments grow under the freeway along the boulevard. Traffic moves slowly on this section of roadway so you notice the details. People sleep on the ground in deplorable conditions with the most minimal shelters made of trash. In the middle of this rubble, you occasionally see a small spark of humanity. An umbrella from a high-end hotel peeking out of a ramshackle structure, a pet dashing by, or a splash of color tying together a whimsical decor will act as momentary reprieves from this scene of misery. These images of suffering have stayed with me. The suffering I have seen and continue to see motivated my decision to use our foundation as a catalyst to sponsor an educational design program to bring some dignity to the lives of the homeless and start getting them off the ground.

One of the most delightful experiences is to witness the flow of creative ideas that come from the young people involved with design education. When those ideas are channeled toward addressing urban issues that confront our cities, it adds a particular relevance to the educational process. I am proud of our foundation's ability to get these innovative thoughts out of the portfolio stage and into the broader public realm. Our experience with the Sanke urban furniture project that now exists on the plaza at the Museum of Contemporary Art, fueled our interest in tackling design problems with a greater social impact.

The genius of the MADWORKSHOP Homeless Studio began with the idea of harnessing the creative spirit that exists around the educational process of design. I fully understand that problems surrounding homelessness are not simple. However, through creative problem solving we can sponsor ideas that can make small but meaningful differences. We approached Qingyun Ma, the former Dean at the USC School of Architecture, with the idea for this class and he brought in his directors at the time, Gail Borden and Hadrian Predock. The University embraced the idea with full enthusiasm. Professor R. Scott Mitchell, one of our trusted Board Members, became involved and the directors brought in Sofia Borges, who is now part of our foundation team, to co-teach with Mitchell. This partnership became the genesis of the class. The class soon took on a life of its own, becoming instrumental in bringing new perspectives to the issue. I am particularly proud that our foundation sparked this remarkable outcome and through design, helped tackle such critical and universal urban issues.

Mary K. Martin
MADWORKSHOP Co-Founder

Our foundation is about two years old now. We have had a number of projects that to us have been very successful. The MADWORKSHOP Homeless Studio has to date been the most visible and the most successful of our efforts. This success in part happened because the subject matter of homelessness is important, very visible, and because of that visibility, very topical. Beyond that, the MADWORKSHOP Homeless Studio is successful because of the pure creative energy put in by the two professors, Sofia Borges and R. Scott Mitchell and the highly motivated and spirited class of students. The fact that the University of Southern California School of Architecture was fully supportive made the environment for success even more possible. The project may be over in the classroom but we are still working with the city of LA and the Mayor's office to build our first proof of concept facility.

Not for a moment did any of us believe that the total cure of homelessness was somehow linked to a single architectural solution. We realized the problem was vast, complicated, and extended well beyond the perspective of the design community. Our first realization was that a permanent housing solution combined with meaningful care to deal with a variety of social and psychological human needs is the formula to end homelessness. As designers, we posses skills that can bring a level of humaneness to the situation. We could be inventive, creating minimal temporary environments that have an element of safety, security, and dignity.

The second step was to recognize that permanent housing takes a long time to implement. Financing, real estate acquisition, building codes, and zoning codes are all detrimental to immediate solutions. If everything goes well, the building timeframe can take up to five years in the city of LA. And yet, the problem is immediate and growing rapidly. Each night nearly 60,000 people sleep on the streets of LA (that we know about). Our approach was to create temporary crisis housing with a degree of sophistication in terms of both humanity and design. Temporary shelter, as it turns out, proves far less complicated and expensive than permanent housing. Temporary shelter can also be mobile. Much of the innovation of the Homes for Hope design comes from the ability to be moved from site to available site. Nobody wants a homeless shelter in their neighborhood. The notion that a shelter doesn't have to be permanent and will never burden a given neighborhood for more than a year or two makes it far more palatable to the NIMBY attitude.

The topic of homelessness was and is too urgent to design a speculative solution around. We decided to involve top city officials and the Departments of Building and Safety and City Planning from the early

inception of the project. They came to school and we went to City Hall. This back and forth dialogue had a number of positive outcomes. City officials offered specific creative "work arounds" for code issues that would throw the project into time consuming building and planning department review. In return, the students showed the sympathetic officials the difficult problems associated with providing minimal shelter. The mass produceable units are designed with highly practical, easily implementable construction techniques that make it possible to manufacture locally. The final incarnation of Homes for Hope stands ready for implementation and enjoys the support of the city all the way up to the Mayor's Office. This overwhelming support from the city was the result of a diligent collaboration, underscoring the importance of bringing others into the conversation and not designing in a vacuum.

By funding this course, Mary and I learned about homelessness in a far more intimate way than we anticipated. One of the major learning and eye opening experiences that will stay with us was attending the three week bootcamp that Sofia and Scott put the students through at the beginning of the semester. There were visits to encampments and service providers. Experts from around California were brought in to communicate the complex nature of the problem. As architects, designers, students, and educators, we have the resources at our disposal to rethink shelter. Homes for Hope and the efforts of the MADWORKSHOP Homeless Studio take the first steps toward that rethinking.

David C. Martin
MADWORKSHOP Co-Founder

My involvement in Homes for Hope began with a phone call in the spring of 2016. Mary and David Martin, the founders of MADWORKSHOP, had a question. They asked if students from the USC School of Architecture might be able to create a practical solution to combat the crisis of homelessness in Los Angeles. A better question could not have been asked and a better opportunity could not have been offered. For years I had been working to provide an outlet for student interest in design/build and fabrication. While the drive is often there, most architectural programs offer limited options in this arena. Simply put, students want to build things and the opportunity for them to tackle real world problems and foster client relationships is almost nonexistent. This disconnect further widens the divide between those who can afford the services of an architect and the traditionally underserved who actually need it the most.

It was clear that the MADWORKSHOP Homeless studio would generate a heavy workload for both faculty and students. Much to my relief I was partnered with Sofia Borges as my co-instructor. While I had not known Sofia personally, I did know her work. It was clear that she was invested and could offer the students an insight into the conversation that I, at the time, could not. The emotional language to discuss the true nature and long-term effects of homelessness was just not there for me. It would take a minute for me to finally comprehend the full scope of the humanitarian crisis we were looking to solve. From our first planning meeting I was convinced that the output from this studio would have a life beyond USC. It was a truly complimentary pairing, that became an ongoing partnership. There was no question that teaching the design/build elements of this course would be grueling. However, I found the most difficult details to be far less tangible. How do you make sure that a student's work is driven by empathy and compassion when you're unclear of your own motivations? Most of the design courses I teach are clinical or technical in nature, and I have, on occasion, been described using those same terms. I knew that this was an opportunity to work outside my normal parameters. It's not an exaggeration to say the project changed me. Prior to this project, I had no real thoughts on ending homelessness. It had simply never been my fight. As Sofia and I developed the Homeless Studio it became apparent that all of my past work and research dovetailed perfectly into the program we were assembling. Someone once told me I was too dirty to work in architecture. I think the comment came in response to my desire to be in a shop, or on site, rather than sitting in an office. It was meant to be a damning assessment, but I took it as a compliment. My first visits to Skid Row gave me a new sense of homelessness as an immediate human crisis—one that I was increasingly sure we could help with. Our group of fourth year undergraduate architecture students, having little, or no, prior experience with either homelessness or practical fabrication, would hit the ground running, from day one. They were not intimidated. In fact, it was stunning to see how quickly they took to the work and how far they were able to push themselves in just fifteen weeks. The balance of research, design and building created an atmosphere of accomplishment. The obvious human impact of their work motivated them even further.

While the studio was meant to cover a lot of ground, we had no idea that it would gain external momentum so early on. Looking back, the request of MADWORKSHOP was perfectly timed as people were looking for answers and open to new ideas. Throughout the process we found government agencies and non-profits eager to help and quick to act. When we reached out, they responded. If an agency couldn't help us, they got us to one who could. The waters of bureaucracy parted before us and the City of Los Angeles was there waiting. City Planning, the Department of Building and Safety and the Mayor's office could not have been more accommodating. Homes for Hope would not have been possible without their direct assistance. Ken Craft, at Hope of the Valley Rescue Mission was an invaluable client and partner from the start.

We have reached a critical point in the struggle to end homelessness. Los Angeles is by no means alone in the crisis. However, rapid growth, gentrification and redevelopment issues specific to the region have made the task far more difficult. With the recent passage of Proposition HHH and Measure H in Los Angeles we have a rare opportunity to fund long-term solutions. The problem now is the phrase "long-term solutions." This permanent supportive housing is in short supply and new projects can take up to five years to complete. Simply navigating the entitlements process can take two years before construction can even begin. Our intent with Homes for Hope was to quickly fill the transitional gap between the street and that permanent home. Effectively reducing the emergency stabilization time frame from years to weeks. Folks like the concept of Homes for Hope. It is safe, structural, modular, efficient, and inexpensive. However, the key selling point is that it's temporary and factory built. Factory built means that no city plan check is required and if we keep the number of habitable units under thirty (30) we avoid the need for a conditional use permit (CUPS). No longer can we sit idly by on the sidelines and call this a policy problem. The entire design community—builders, architects, designers, fabricators, and especially students—has an opportunity to help right now and an obligation to do so.

R. Scott Mitchell
Assistant Professor of Architectural Practice, USC
Principal, Gigante AG

MADWORKSHOP

Instructors: R. Scott Mitchell & Sofia Borges

HOMELESS STUDIO

Twenty percent of our country's homeless population live in California.

We see them each day in our peripheral vision—hunkered down at the local bus stop, resting on the stoop next to our favorite coffee shop, or temporarily occupying a transitional space under a rare awning. And while we know these people are there and that they have needs and dreams just like the rest of us, we walk past them, averting our eyes. We have no vision of how to contain the problem so we look away. This collective complicity turns our homeless into urban ghosts. We all know their images and they rightfully haunt us. In 2015, the city of Los Angeles declared a state of emergency on homelessness, casting light on our growing epidemic unrivaled anywhere else in the country.

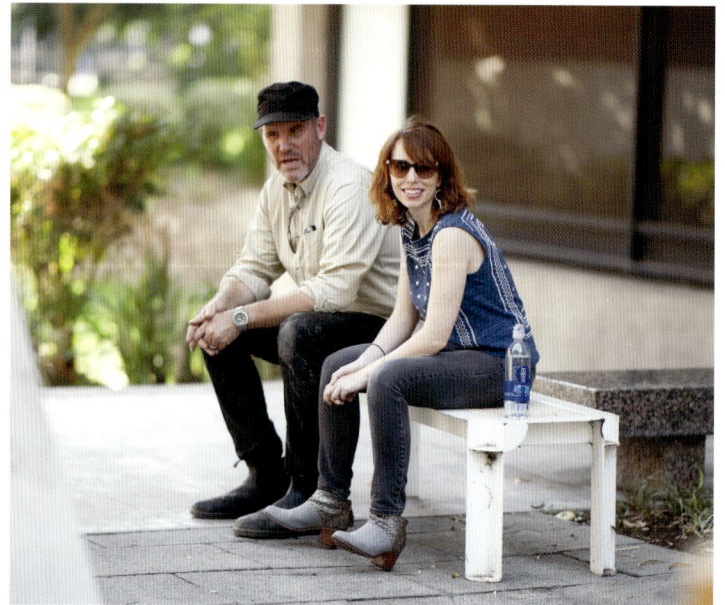

This page: Students presenting at City Hall, course sponsors David and Mary Martin, instructors R. Scott Mitchell and Sofia Borges.

Opposite page: Student Belinda Pak framing a tiny home, Students visiting their client Marvin in an encampment in Vernon, Deputy Mayor of Economic Opportunity Brenda Shockley for the city of Los Angeles shaking hands with students during final review.

Through a gererous grant made by David and Mary Martin, the MADWORKSHOP Homeless Studio spent the Fall of 2016 exploring the architect's role in solving homelessness.

The studio focused specifically on the area of transitional housing, looking at temporary, modular, and expandable solutions. Students gained real world insight into the complexities of the problem, including numerous site visits to key local agencies including the **Skid Row Housing Trust**, **LAMP**, **Downtown Women's Center**, **Midnight Mission**, and more. Students spoke and engaged with the homeless and formerly homeless to learn firsthand about their visions and barriers toward housing. Experts and pioneers on the topic including **Michael Maltzan**, **Ted Hayes**, and **Betty Chinn** joined the class from across California for lectures, discussions, reviews, and hands-on fabrication workshops.

The studio divided into a short charette on nomadic/parasitic structures, followed by a tiny homes fabrication workshop led by the Oakland based artist **Gregory Kloehn**. The second half of the semester was devoted to the design of a temporary housing solution for **Hope of the Valley Rescue Mission** in the San Fernando Valley. Students had the rare opportunity to work directly with CEO Ken Craft to develop thoughtful and imaginative solutions to help the organization manage their increasing number of residents.

The design and fabrication heavy studio included the construction of full-scale prototypes and the completion of a series of tiny homes for the homeless. Throughout the semester, students worked closely with local agencies, city officials, luminaries, artists, and activists to develop a holistic solution to tackling homelessness in Los Angeles through design. The homeless are always thinking about architecture. It's time we started thinking about them.

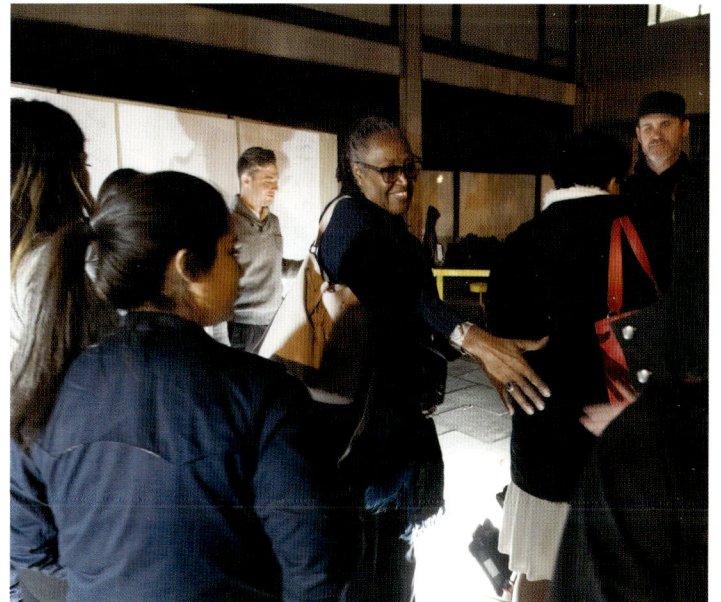

THE BOOT CAMP

It is easy to assume why someone is homeless. Based on that assumption, it is easy to assume you know the proper design solution to help. In order to avoid designing at a distance, the class underwent a three week homelessness boot camp. Organizations such as Skid Row Housing Trust, Downtown Women's Center, The Midnight Mission, and others opened up their doors. Prominent figures from Betty Chinn to Gary Blasi and City Librarian John Szabo to Michael Maltzan all played key roles during this intensive immersion into the topic.

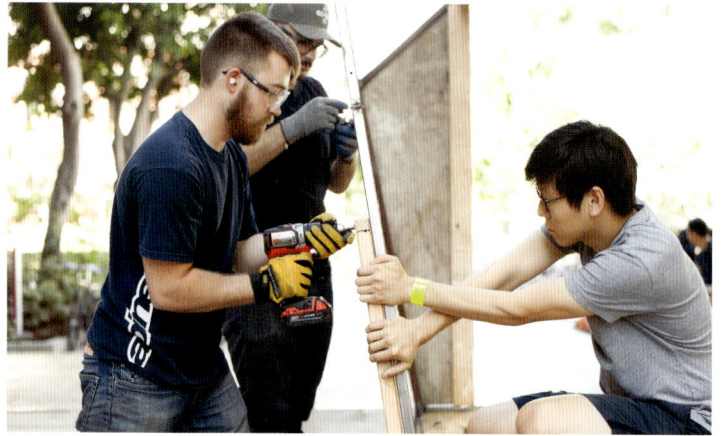

This page: Homeless activisit Ted Hayes consulting with students, Architect Michael Maltzan speaking to students.

Opposite page: A view of Skid Row and downtown Los Angeles from the Midnight Mission.

Discussing Crest Apartments at Michael Maltzan Architecture.

Touring the Midnight Mission's gymnasium and offices with David Prentice.

Louis Tse visiting the classes' nomadic shelters (Photo credit: John Uniack).

SKID ROW HOUSING TRUST

MIKE ALVIDREZ, CEO

"A home, when paired with appropriate support services, is the most effective and compassionate solution to homelessness, and ultimately reduces public costs."

I was born in Los Angeles and have lived here my entire life. I have seen this city transform many times over the decades, and I have witnessed many milestones in the city's history, including the arrival of the Los Angeles Dodgers, the 1984 Olympics, and the construction of the Walt Disney Concert Hall. But Los Angeles has one claim to fame that I find profoundly disturbing: we have the largest population of unsheltered homeless people anywhere in the nation.

I have witnessed growing inequality amongst Angelenos—particularly when it comes to housing. Rents in Los Angeles are now some of the highest in the nation, forcing low-income people to spend more on housing and less on food, clothing, and other necessities. Over the last few decades, wages for low and middle income people have remained stagnant or declined while the cost of basic medical and mental health care has increased. Too many of our neighbors are one crisis away from homelessness, and there is not enough housing and support available to keep people off the streets. Too many people fall through the cracks. Los Angeles has historically reacted to homelessness by criminalizing its most visible symptoms, restricting where people can sleep or how many possessions they can keep. Los Angeles will only turn the tide against homelessness when we proactively address its root causes.

I started working for Skid Row Housing Trust not long after it was founded to preserve affordable housing in Downtown Los Angeles. Skid Row Housing Trust was an early adopter of Housing First, an approach to ending homelessness in which homeless individuals can move directly into a safe and permanent home with an array of voluntary supportive services without barriers such as mandatory sobriety, treatment, or requirements to complete programs. This approach is effective in promoting housing stability, particularly among people who have been homeless for long periods and have serious disabilities or disorders, including addiction. Skid Row Housing Trust currently offers permanent supportive housing—a combination of subsidized housing and comprehensive supportive services—to approximately 1,800 people in Los Angeles. Through housing and support, we have helped thousands of people overcome homelessness who were once considered beyond reach.

Eight years ago, Ed Givens was identified by the Los Angeles County Department of Mental Health as one of the top 50 homeless individuals most likely to die on the streets of Downtown Los Angeles' Skid Row. After being referred to Skid Row Housing Trust's Cobb Apartments, Ed could address the underlying conditions that led him to be homeless, maintain his housing, improve his health and mental health, and reconnect with family and community. If you met Ed today, you would never know that he was once in such a vulnerable situation. Permanent supportive housing transformed his life.

There are thousands of Eds who still struggle to survive on the streets of Skid Row, throughout Los Angeles, and across the entire nation. We identify them as "chronically homeless"—individuals who are homeless for years at a time (in Ed's case, over 25 years) and have a combination of disabling medical and mental health conditions that make it almost impossible for them to access housing independently. A 2016 study found that LA County spends over $1 billion a year caring for and managing people without homes.

The majority ($577 million) went to health needs, another $294 million was for benefits and food stamps, and another $41 million was for law enforcement costs—including arrests by the Sheriff's Department, jail stays, and probation for homeless people. A home, when paired with appropriate support services, is the most effective and compassionate solution to homelessness, and ultimately reduces public costs.

Over our 28-year history, Skid Row Housing Trust has evolved a great deal in its approach to housing development. We have shifted our focus from preservation to new construction, and have embedded social

services and community spaces in each property. Having medical, mental health, recovery, and other supportive services on site makes it easier for residents to regularly access them. Partnering with renowned firms like Michael Maltzan Architecture, Koning Eizenberg Architecture, Killefer Flammang Architects, and Brooks + Scarpa allowed Skid Row Housing Trust to push the standards of permanent supportive housing design. We found that people who have experienced the trauma of extreme poverty and homelessness greatly benefit from thoughtful design that facilitates healing and connection, both within and outside our walls. The design of our buildings challenges common perceptions of subsidized housing, and allows our residents to escape the labels that so often accompany low-income tenants who have experienced homelessness. We use architecture to elevate the conversation about ending homelessness and to inspire stronger communities.

Poverty and homelessness in America are man-made problems, and solving these problems are a matter of political will and investment. I think a better city is possible, one in which affordable housing and critical supportive services like health care, mental health care, and substance use recovery are readily available to anyone in need. That will be a Los Angeles that we can all be proud to call home.

Previous page: Skid Row Housing Trust's Heidi Genrich, Mike Alvidrez, and Anne Dobson at their New Pershing Apartments.

Below: Rachel Kassenbrock of Downtown Women's Center discusses MADWORKSHOP Homeless Studio's Homes for Hope with Heidi Genrich and Anne Dobson.

Opposite Page: The Six Apartments by Michael Maltzan (Photo Credit: Tara Wujcik).

TED HAYES

"Homeless are more affected by the environment than anyone."

In 1984, Ted Hayes decided that the best way to help the homeless was to become homeless himself. During his time on the streets, Ted founded Justiceville and Dome Village—the first organized homeless communities of their kind. Although dismantled in 2006, Dome Village remains the longest standing, self-governed homeless collective in Los Angeles to this day.

What started your journey into the world of homelessness?

TH: Dr. King coined the universal idea that we are to judge ourselves not by our outward appearances, races, and so forth, but by the content of our character. I was brought up in a family that cared about other people. My mother and father always taught us to stand up for people who cannot stand up for themselves. I carried that idea all the way through high school and almost became the first black senior class president of my town in 1969. But I decided not to run. Instead I helped someone else win. I wanted to have a committee in student council that represented the C-D-E-F students, the underperforming students, the bad guys, the smokers in the bathroom, the outcasts. You know, guys like me. And I got it. And I built a link to the Mayor and called it "The Grievance Committee." Then I became very spiritual. I always fussed and complained about what's wrong with the world. We all talk about what we see is wrong but we never offer solutions. We expect other people to come up with the solutions of what we criticize. I realized that if I care so much about the poor and the homeless, I needed to go be with them. Fix it myself. So I left my family and went to downtown LA, and saw the tent city of 1984/85 that was started by Harry Rogers, who would become one of my mentors. It was the Christmas holiday season. There were two big white tents across the street from the *LA Times* building and City Hall. The moment I got there I had an epiphany that this was going to be my work for the rest of my life. So I began to sleep on the sidewalks. That's when Justiceville was born. Justiceville was the first organized encampment politically. The idea was to empower the people. Not give them a handout or hand up but to empower their hands to do for themselves and for others. And it was working!

We had designed a transitional housing concept of geodesic domes with Buckminster Fuller's grandson Jamie Snyder. He came to Justiceville and we became friends. Jamie had heard about us in the news and we were talking about using domes as an idea for transitional housing. So he came down to Skid Row! Clean cut, white dude. And he came

down, no fear, no nothing, and sat right there in the encampment with us. He ate with us, we hung out. And he said, "You guys are on to something. We'd love to help you out." About this time a guy named Craig Chamberlain, a Vietnam vet who studied under Bucky Fuller, showed up. I thought, "this guy's a genius!" He created the 'Omnisphere' off of Bucky Fuller's Geodesic Dome. Jamie Snyder had a Geodesic Dome at his house in the Palisades that Craig had designed. He let us use that for a reception.

We had created a microcosm. We had cleaned up the street between 5th and 6th Street on Gladys Avenue. That's where we were. Right next door to the "The Hippie Kitchen," the Catholic Workers Kitchen where they feed the homeless. We camped there. We were in the news all the time. We could call press conferences. We were the darling of the press. We had a telephone put in and a camping shack. We got four sanitary companies to set up four toilets for us. We cleaned up the alleyway and put up these toilets and secured them. We even started an auto detailing business. But by the time we really got going, the local social services providers went to Mayor Tom Bradley, the first black mayor of Los Angeles, and said "you need to shut that down." And Tom Bradley said "I can't shut it down. I have nothing to do with that." And they said, "How about going to the County then? And getting to the property owner..." His name was Ernie Doizaki. He was a great hero to us. He had inherited the American Fish Company downtown from his dad and when we found out that he owned the property we asked him if we could stay there for one dollar per year. He said yes. He loved what we were doing, we cleaned the neighborhood up.

Why did people want to shut down Justiceville?

TH: If you think about it, we're talking about strengthening the hands of the poor. In other words, people need the poor and the homeless to feel good about themselves. And we threatened the whole system. They knew that if people became self-sufficient that there'd be no more need for food kitchens, transitional housing, dome villages, tiny houses, any of this stuff. So they shut it down. They told the County to go see Ernie Doizaki and tell Ernie, "If you don't evict these people, were going to run a health inspection on your food factory. And you will not pass." So Ernie got spooked and he called me up and I said, "Don't worry. Go ahead and evict us. We will always speak highly of you, but we have to be arrested." He agreed and he came down the day of the eviction. Police everywhere, helicopters, news cameras...I'd never seen so much press in my life. And there we were. A federal judge called up Daryl Gates, the police chief at the time and a legendary "bad cop," and said that they were watching the procedures and that he better not harm us. This was pre-Rodney King. LAPD already had a bad reputation then. So when they came to arrest us, we walked out of Justiceville with our hands up.

What was the assimilation process like starting as an outsider and ending up as a leader of a group of people who were not homeless by choice like you but by necessity?

TH: It was scary. I've never been so scared in my life. It was just me now. I had to get used to sleeping on the sidewalk and in unsafe situations. We had to cover our heads with our blankets because of the rats running by all night long. You have to get used to the hygiene of the streets. You can go for days, weeks, without water or a change of clothes. The people that eat out of garbage cans eat there because they'd rather not wait in the food lines. And you think "how are you gonna eat garbage?" Well, you acclimate. I had never slept on a hard sidewalk in my life. But after a while, I could sleep anywhere.

Eventually I had friends where I could go get a shower, a good night's sleep. Or I'd go visit my family in Riverside. You need those outlets.

How did you get people to trust you and to start looking to you for guidance and leadership?

TH: I served them. I was the Servant Director of Justiceville. I cleaned up trash, paper...I washed their dishes. I'd be up til 2:30am some nights doing that stuff. I'd do security for them, make sure they'd sleep at night. I'd go get food, bring it in. Firewood. It got to the point where people began to wonder, "who is this guy?" I didn't talk to them, I'd just do the work. Cause I knew, you don't just walk in, you don't know these people, and they don't know you. So I won them over. They trusted me. I knew it was really starting to happen one night around the campfire. I was talking about my philosophy, and they were listening. One guy started to interrupt and the others stopped him, "Quiet! Ted's talking!" It got to the point where I led the meetings. They wanted to call me their king

Above: Ted constructing Dome Village circa 1993.

but I said "I'm not here to be your king. I'm here to be your servant. And I expect you to serve one another." That's how I got my leadership.

How long did that take?

TH: Maybe a couple of months. It's tribal. The leadership came because I earned it. But it's hard to come out once you've transitioned into that world. You've found freedom. You do what you want to do.

How did you locate Ernie's land?

TH: It was a vacant lot. It used to be a playground for children. Tires and sand. It was run by a teenage Latino gang called 'The Flats.' So when we got to the property we tried to find the owner. We went to his office and introduced ourselves. We told him what we were doing and he said "I like what you're doing. The street's cleaner..." But it started out as a random site.

How long did Justiceville last?

TH: Five months. From January 2nd to May 10th of 1985.

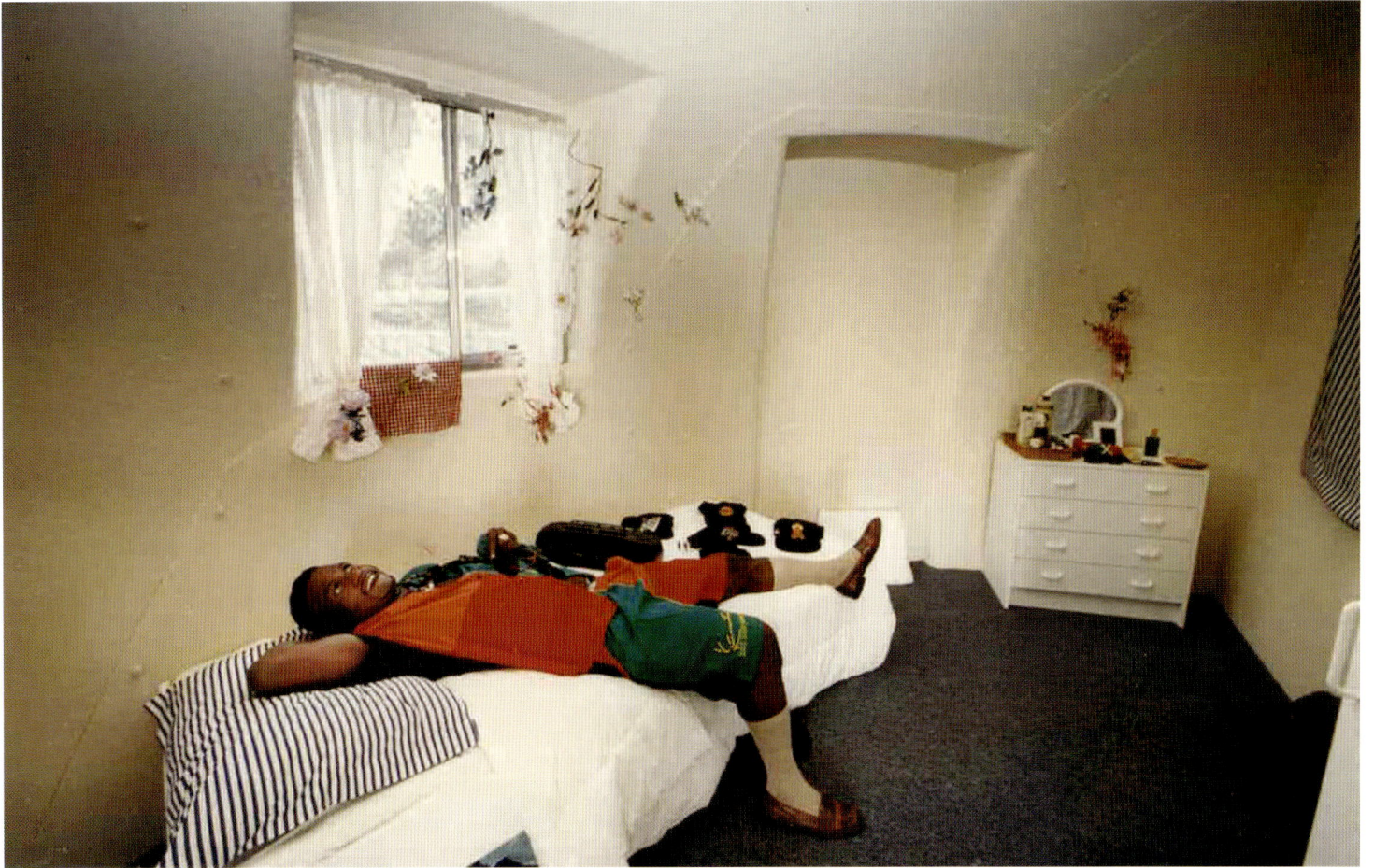

How many residents lived in Justiceville?

TH: It got up to about 73 residents. Men, women, children, pets. We were all there. Overcrowded. It was a very small lot compared to where we moved next.

You could fit Justiceville into Dome Village three or four times. Almost half of the population was Hispanic.

How did you decide who got to be a resident of Justiceville? What was that process like?

TH: If someone wanted to come in, we'd make space. As long as you followed our guidelines—participate in doing chores, keep your area clean, help with nighttime security. We were unlike all the other shelters because you didn't have to be drug-free to come in here. We'd work with you. But you can't cause trouble.

You've spoken about the importance of not having temporary solutions become permanent ones. If Justiceville hadn't been cut short, how would people have cycled through this community?

TH: It was primitive back then but when I went into homelessness, I did it consciously. I'm a civil rights activist. I had known for years that the US military had shut down hundreds of military bases across the country. The key to ending homelessness is space, land. We have the space, let's use it. I've always believed that we have to decentralize our urban centers around the world if humanity is going to survive. And homeless people, their condition warrants the ability to get up and move. They don't have roots like other people have. The poorest people go first and then we follow. That's always how it's been. Justiceville and Dome Village were only temporary. These were a way station, a temporary stop. We must keep moving. We don't need anymore programs. We need an end to the programs. But people keep giving money and there are more homeless and more programs. Why? Because there are no places to put these people. Do you want them in your neighborhood? No! "I'll give you a check to put them in their neighborhood!" [points in the other direction] And I understand that. I don't condemn people for being NIMBYs. The homeless can be NIMBYs too. We exist on a much more primordial, primitive plane of existence. We don't think about tomorrow. We think about right now. But I knew going in that we were going to have to resolve homelessness. We were going to have to have an exiting process to transition people out of this world and into the next.

What happened after your eviction from Justiceville?

TH: We became urban nomads. We would travel from spot to spot looking for new vacant areas. We'd camp out, the police would come and chase us off. We'd go somewhere else, they'd chase us off. Until one day we went over to Crown Hill, now some of the most expensive land in the city. It was a great place to camp. We were out of sight and surrounded by flowers, bushes, trees....From there we'd go down into the city to do our lobbying. One day, a Herald Examiner reporter found us. He wanted to do an exclusive story. I said, "Ok but you must not tell where we are." And of course this knucklehead told the press. The property owner came out and said, "I know you guys are here, I know who you are. I've heard about Ernie...So just be quiet." But then it hits the newspapers and we've gotta go. So the police came and three of us got arrested. Two army veterans and me. And we went to court. We still stayed on sidewalks and streets but we just kept moving around town. We never could find a decent place. Eventually we found the Bradbury Building where we worked out of for a while.

During this time we went to trial. When we'd do an act of civil disobedience we wanted to get to court to present our case to the public. Jim Hahn, the City Attorney, knew this and would always arrest us, smack us on the hand, and let us go. This particular time, he decided to prosecute us. And we were like "Thank you!"

You wanted to go to jail?

TH: Yeah, man! Trespassing! If we went to jail, our story gets out there. We won that court case. The ACLU got involved, and we whipped that DA bad. We were found not guilty. That was the beginning of what you see downtown and all across the city. We won our case on the defense of necessity. We began by saying, "Your honor, ladies and gentlemen of the jury, yes the streets are a bad place to live. Yes, the sidewalks are filthy and dangerous. Yes, you're right about all of this and it's oftentimes trespassing." But then we started painting the pictures of the missions and the shelters, and how bad that is...what's going on in the hotels...And they realized that we were better off in the streets, the sidewalks, and the encampments than in those shelters. So that created more red tape in the city about how to approach homeless encampments. About a year and a half later, we would camp out where the old tent city was across the street from the LA Times building in that vacant lot. In the daytime, we'd leave the lot and go to City Hall. We'd line up all of our shopping carts very neatly and leave two people there to do security. The rest of us would go out foraging and doing our activism. Well I went home to my family for the weekend to get a rest. When I get back they tell me the police came with the city management and they took everything and threw it in the garbage. So we ran to City Council and they got on Tom Bradley. Suddenly we're meeting with all these big guns. Attorney Jim Davis found out about us, great guy, legendary, and he came to our rescue. We sued the city. Settled out of court. Each person got $500. This created more stringent laws about how you approach homeless encampments. What's starting to happen now is homeless people are feeling a little bit more emboldened about encamping. Then we had another case. That's when the ACLU and all the other activists realized that we've got something here. That's why to this day, Mayor Garcetti has told the police to stand down. Do not harass the homeless encampments. You can't touch 'em because of what we did.

We put the tiny homes that you came to see in an encampment in Vernon. A couple of weeks later, the city came and bulldozed the encampment, tiny homes and all. Why do you think that happened?

TH: Rogue actions still happen, but you can't do that kind of thing downtown. Isolated encampments are still vulnerable. You're not protected out there. Probably the neighborhood didn't want it. But there are guidelines that have to be followed before you can do that. You've gotta post the warning signs, you've gotta go talk to them, you've gotta send in social service providers to help find them a place to live...But places that are kind of out there, what happened at your encampment can still happen. But you can't touch them downtown. You can't touch them in Venice. You can't touch them in Santa Monica... some places in Beverly Hills. I'm starting to call them "the untouchables." They have more right than you do. We warned the city. We warned Tom Bradley. We warned Richard Riordan. We warned all of them. We gave them the blueprint and said "If you don't implement this or something like this, you're going to have a big problem." Where are these people going to go? There are more people falling into homelessness than leaving. You're creating a stagnant pond here. Homelessness is not going to get better. It only stands to get worse. Even people with money cannot find housing.

How did you start working in the Bradbury Building?

TH: We stayed on the 3rd floor for a couple of months. One of our allies downtown in the Business Improvement District told us that there was some space in the building and talked to them on our behalf. Homeless people in the Bradbury Building? [laughs]

How did Dome Village finally get launched?

TH: One day, we saw a news interview with David V. Adams, the owner of the TWA building on Wilshire Blvd. He had to remove some homeless people from his property and he was saying that he didn't want to do it, that these people needed a place to go. He cared. So I called him up. The next morning we had a meeting and I told him all of my ideas. His response was, "You need a business credibility partner. And that's me. We're going to do your Dome Village." He gave us an office space. Built us a board. Helped us find the property between 8th and 9th St on the East Side of the 110 freeway two blocks from where Staples Center is now. There was already an encampment out front in the cul de sac. We found out who the property owner was and met with him. Arco president and Chairman of the Board Lod Cook tracked me down and I went to speak to him and his board about our ideas. He asked me how much we needed. I said $250,000. He wrote me a check right there. That paid for the domes, platforms, electricity, and the first few months of operations. From there, Dome Village was maintained by a mixture of Federal, state, and city funding, donations, and volunteers. Then we went to Mayor Richard Riordan and told him we got the money and the property. So he helped us get the Department of Building and Safety on board. And to everyone's chagrin, we did the impossible. They put the bar so high that no one could reach it.

But we had the plans. Now we had the money, which we started investing into the domes. This was around 1992/93. We were almost ready to break ground on Dome Village and I decided to run for mayor. Dome Village was a main part of my platform. That's how I met Richard Riordan and why he helped us out when the time came.

How many domes were in Dome Village?

TH: Twenty.

How did you deal with capacity?

TH: We never had more than thirty people at a time, plus pets. You want to maintain a sense of community. When you have those big facilities, nobody knows anyone. If you create the proper environment, people can figure things out for themselves. But never give freedom to human beings. They will not value it. You make them earn freedom. We had to change our rules and make the people earn the privilege to live in Dome Village. Then we had more order. People stayed from a year to 18 months.

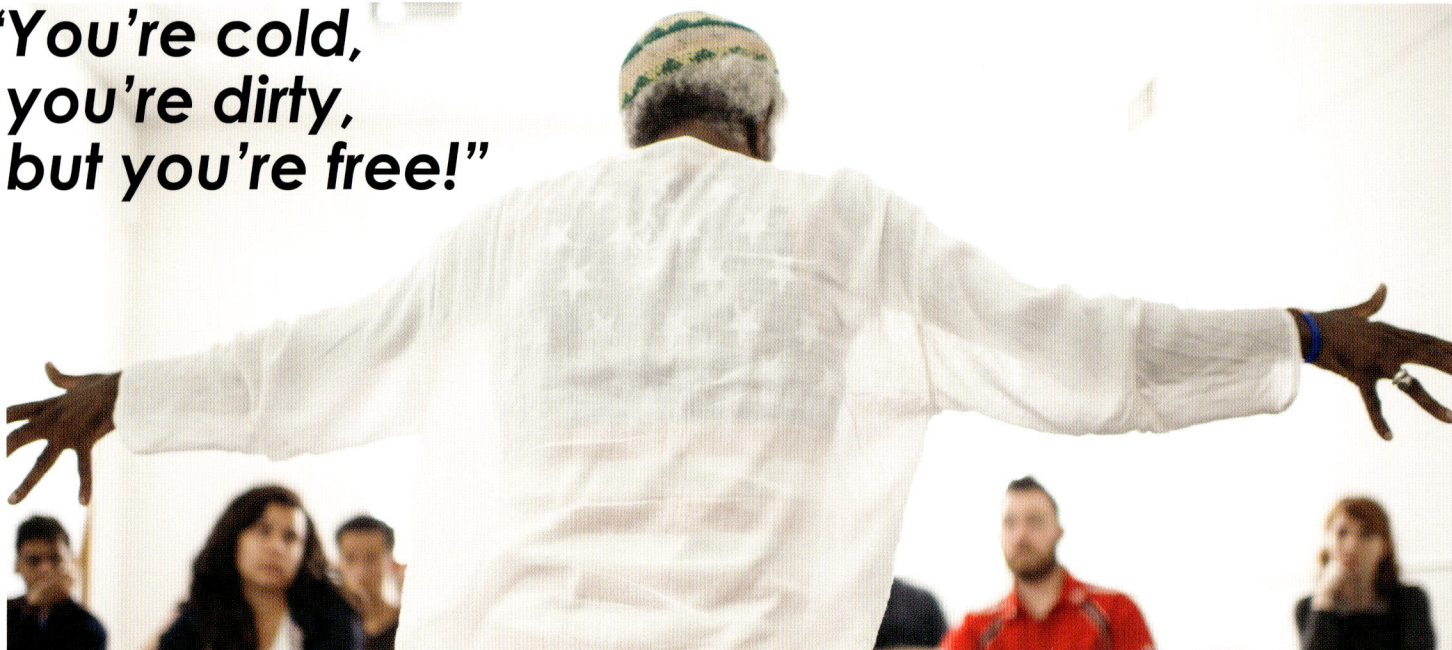

"You're cold, you're dirty, but you're free!"

Above: Ted Hayes speaking to the MADWORKSHOP Homeless Studio at USC. **Right:** Dome Village in its heyday (Dome Village photos courtesy of Ted Hayes).

How did you pick who would live there?

TH: Ronda Flazbaum was the main person that screened people. She was the program director. We couldn't take people with really serious mental issues. We didn't have the proper facilities for them. The people we could accept had to function within the community at a basic level. We had limits.

Did you have plumbing?

TH: Yes, in the kitchen, the showers, and the laundry dome. We had a shared kitchen and shower facility. We had a bathroom facility for women and one for men, wheelchair accessible.

What kind of programs did you have on-site?

TH: We had a garden club. We had a cyber dome. People would donate computers to us and we had internet there in Dome Village in the mid 1990s. People would come in from the surrounding community for our internet access, computer classes, word processing classes. We had holiday events to engage low income communities. We had a health fair, community cleanups. We had a community center, a skate club...Tree plantings. The Compton Cricket Club. We let the homeless give back to the community. Imagine that.

How did you see Dome Village evolving over time?

TH: Dome Village was supposed to last no more than three years. Ideally there would have been several Dome Villages constantly moving across the city like a vacuum cleaner. We'd pick people up off the streets, stabilize them, and them move them to a large facility elsewhere to begin the resocialization process out of homelessness. We did not want to be a burden on anyone's community. Put it down, move it. Put it down, move it. That's how it was supposed to go. But we got blocked. And for thirteen years we languished on that same corner. That was not supposed to happen. I was so happy when the property owner finally said "I want you out of here," and raised our rent from $2,500 to $18,000 a month. That was 2006. I was done with this.

What happened to the domes?

TH: At first we thought about moving the whole thing but we ended up selling most of them on eBay. $3,000 a piece.

If the communities you built had lasted, what were you planning next?

TH: We probably would have had a lot more Dome Villages. We should have been done by now. All this work was 30 years ago. We should have solved homelessness in America and been moving on to helping solve it in other countries. If we can create a model that works in this country, everybody will follow.

NOMADIC SHELTERS

An average person in the United States moves 11.4 times in a lifetime. The average homeless person in the United States can easily move this many times in the course of a single week. Imagine having to pack up your life and relocate several times a day for the indefinite future. How would a forced nomadic lifestyle influence your relationship to belongings and architecture? Where would you gravitate toward? What would you build from? What belongings would become the most indispensable for your survival and comfort?

The homeless are master builders. When the city seizes their shelter, they rebuild. When the weather changes, they modify. The architectural typology of homelessness thrives on ingenuity, pragmatism, and adaptation. People experiencing homelessness work quickly with salvaged materials, carving out fleeting and private interstitial spaces within the public realm.

For this first project, the students worked in small groups to develop full scale, occupiable, nomadic shelters. This was the first time that many of the students had ever built anything. The shelter designs are collapsible, compassionate, and can be reconfigured to adapt to a range of locations. The designs build off of the vernaculars and materials readily found on the streets of Los Angeles.

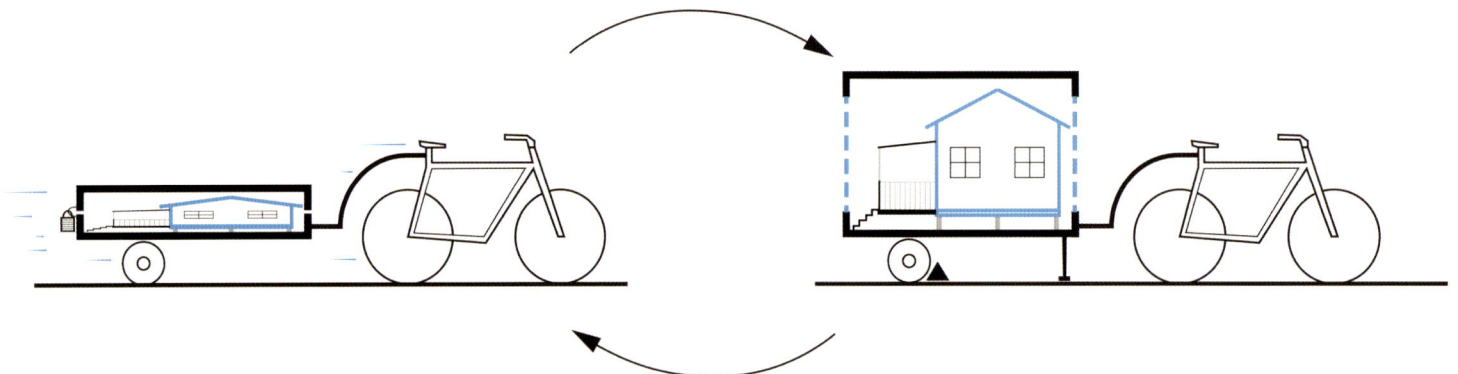

ROLLY

Maria Ceja & Alexxa Solomon

The Rolly is a portable shelter that is three feet and two inches wide, and three feet and four inches tall. These dimensions are comparable to those of a shopping cart. This shelter was designed to easily navigate sidewalks and doors. There is no need for additional equipment to move Rolly, it is moveable with just two hands able to push.

Low cost and efficient, the Rolly can be produced with just wood and sustainable coroplast sheets.

When on the move, the cart is just a box. As soon as the cart is stationed, the bed can fold down and the collapsible dome shelter can be pulled down by the rope handle. To transform Rolly, from just being a cart to a home, the collapsible shelter can be slid up or down when in need of privacy, ventilation, or even when simply wanting to look up at the stars. A frosted skylight was also incorporated into the cart, for an additional light source when the dome is completely shut.

This easy compact shelter not only provides a moveable sleeping space, but an opportunity for home while on the streets.

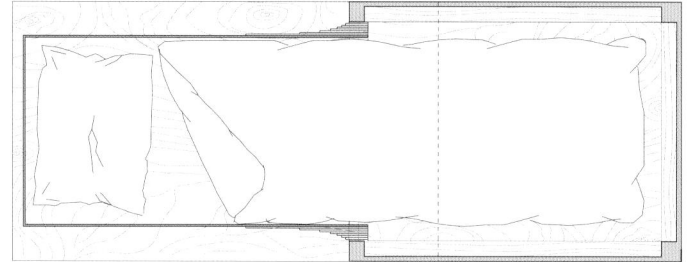

PLAN @1'0"

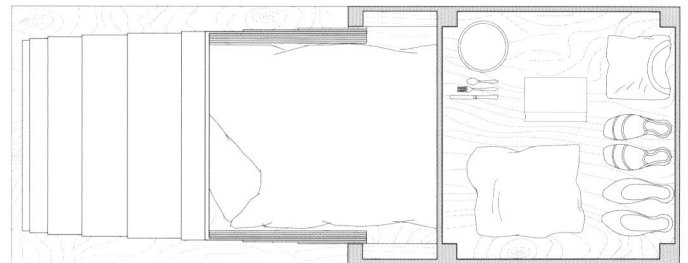

PLAN @2'2"

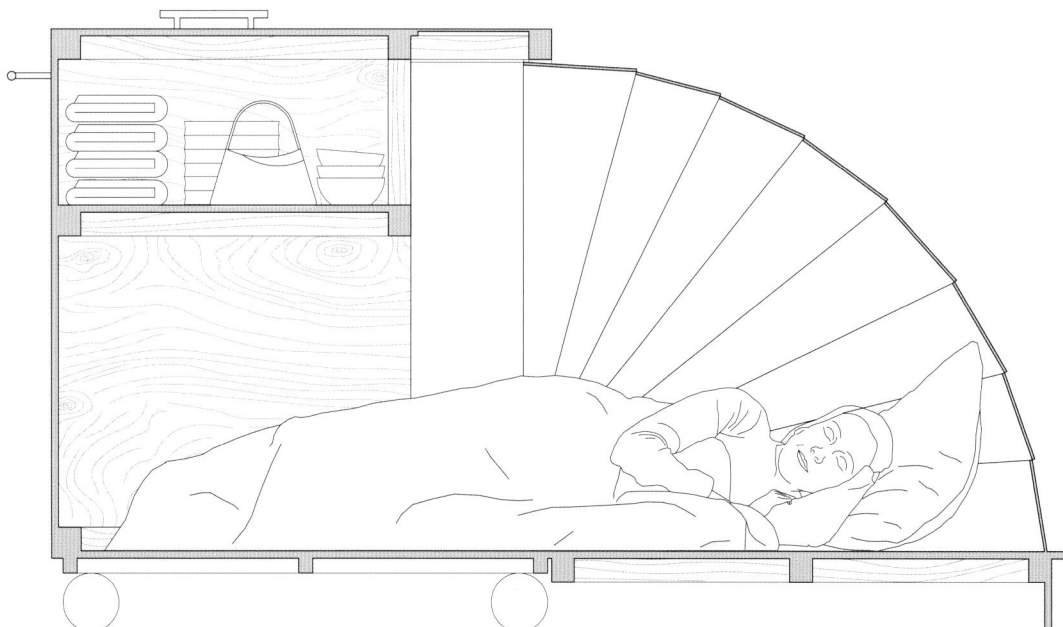

SECTION

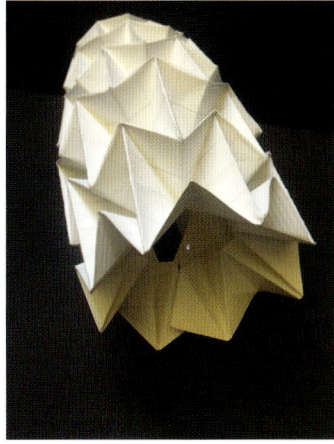

THE ROMAD

Jeremy Carman & Jayson Champlain

The romad provides homeless individuals with an immediate source of shelter, while also allowing the easy mobility of a bike trailer. The shelter provides security, storage, and social spaces, along with the ability to roam, rest, and reside. These mobile homes support nomadic tendencies with a three step system of deployment. By physically lifting a homeless individual off the street in an elevated sleeping cot, and adding an extendable deck that becomes a front porch, the resident has the chance to take a breath, collect themselves, and decide the next best step.

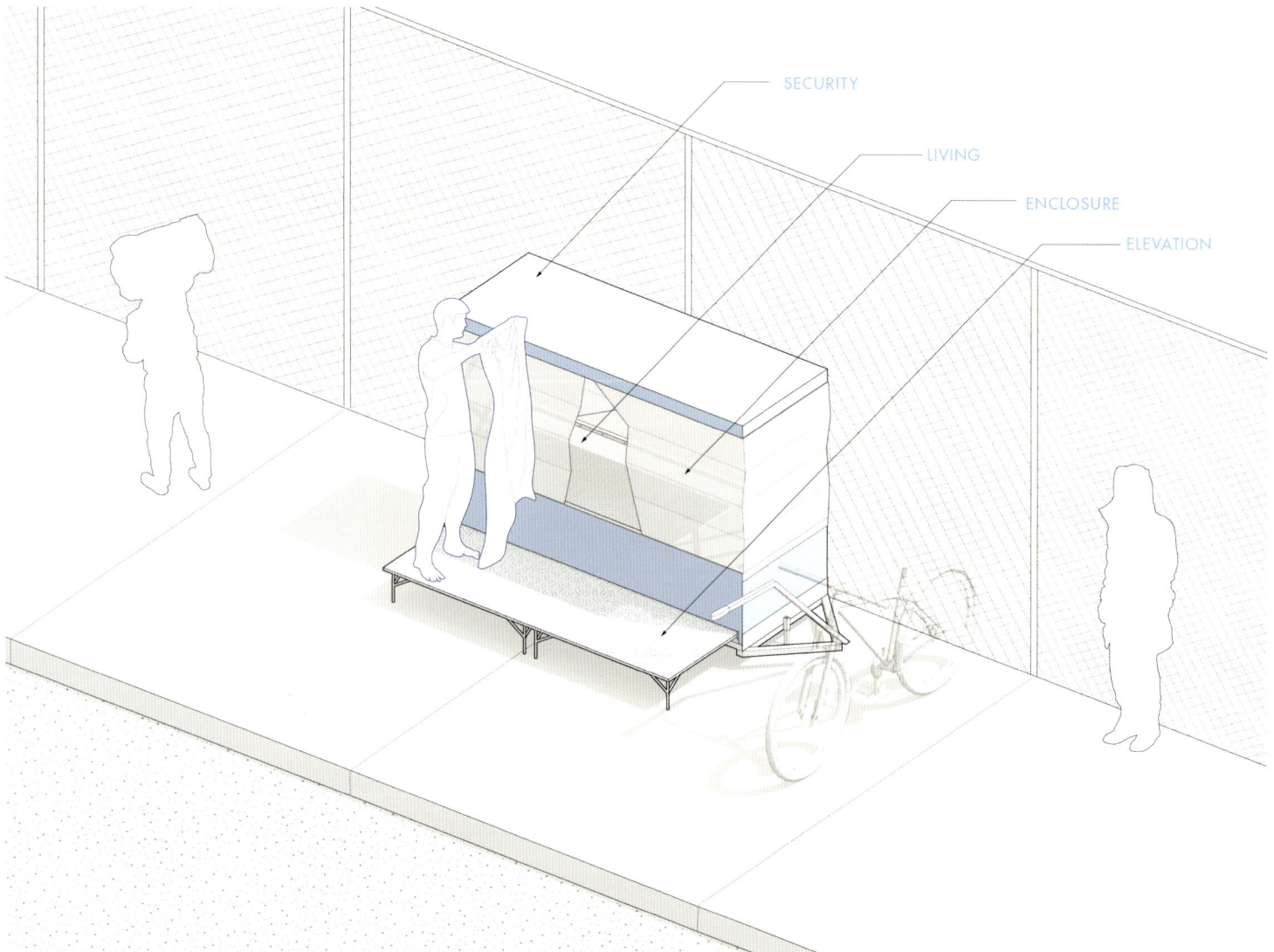

SECURITY

LIVING

ENCLOSURE

ELEVATION

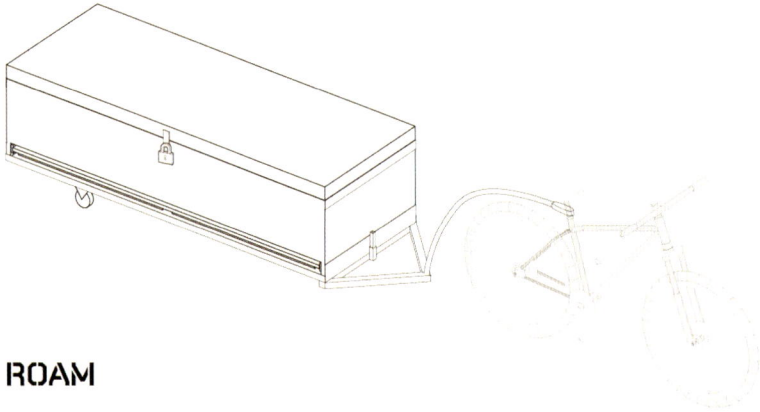

1. ROAM

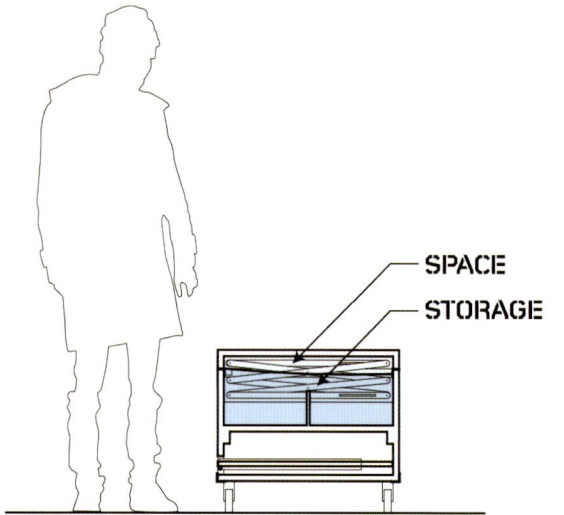

SPACE
STORAGE

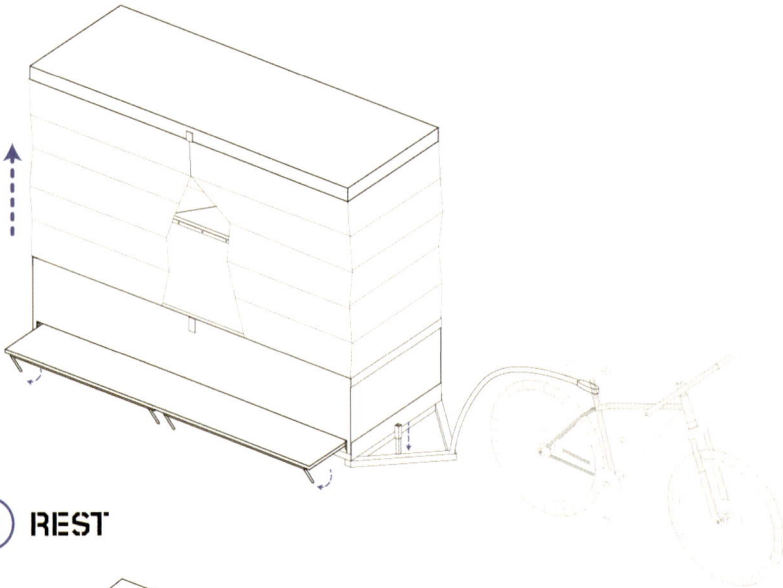

2. REST

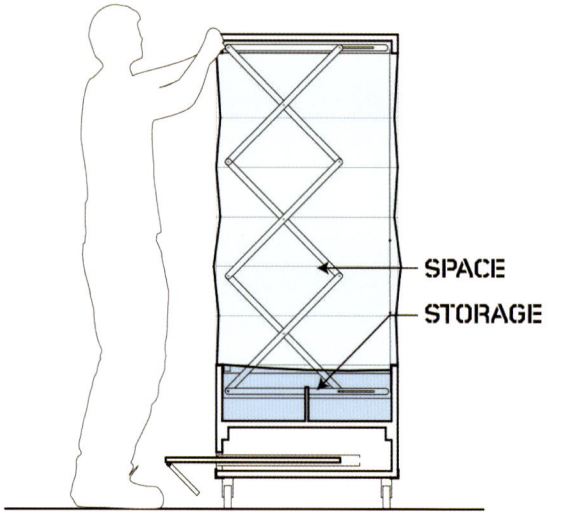

SPACE
STORAGE

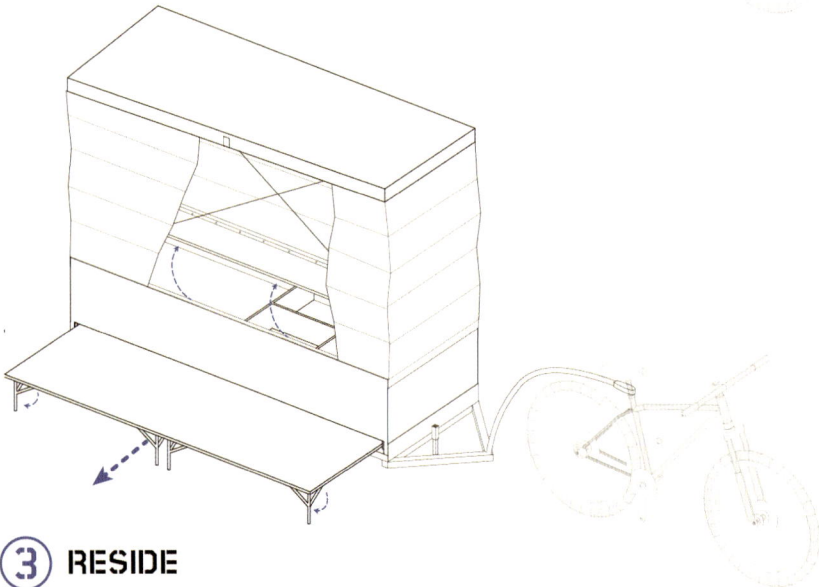

3. RESIDE

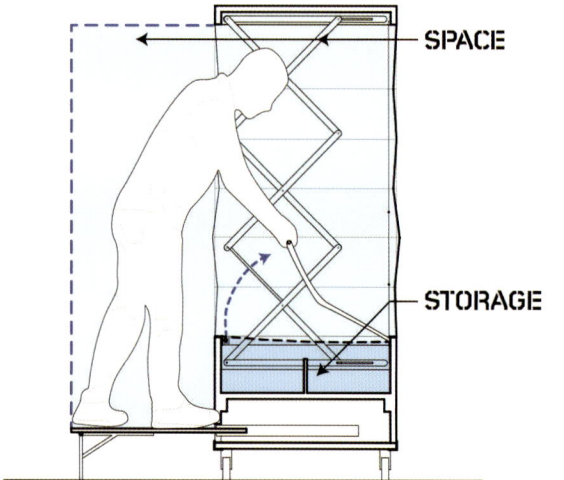

SPACE

STORAGE

TwoCube

Joseph Chang & Heeje Yang

TwoCube is a mobile shelter designed to be compact and yet homey. The shelter is comprised of a cube within a cube that someone experiencing homelessness can easily cart around the sidewalks of Los Angeles and beyond. To store items during the day, simply, open the side door of the exterior cube to reveal a storage compartment inside the interior cube. When stationary, the interior cube can be pulled out of the exterior cube to make an inhabitable space. The interior wood paneled walls provide the user a nook to comfortably sit and sleep in a cozy space. Along with a sliding window, there is a desk area where the occupant can do work, or place personal belongings. When it's time to move to a new location, TwoCube makes it easy. The user only needs to return the bedding material back into its compartment. Then the interior cube is ready to be slid back into place. Drawings, paintings, and pictures can be left on the walls and items on the desk will remain untouched until re-inhabited. TwoCube allows the user to keep their personalized living space when the overall shelter needs to become portable.

46

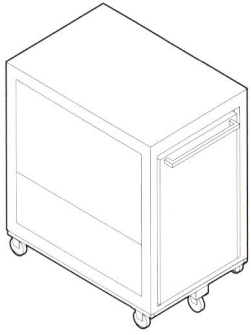
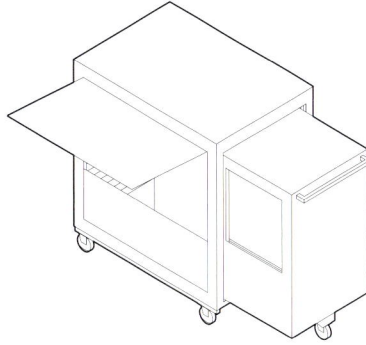
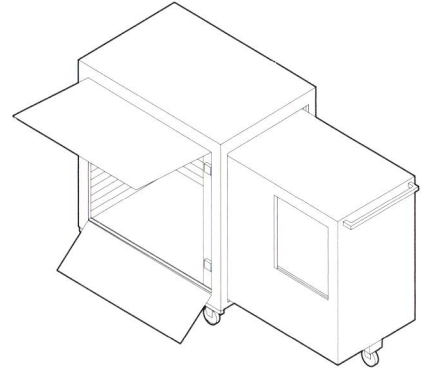

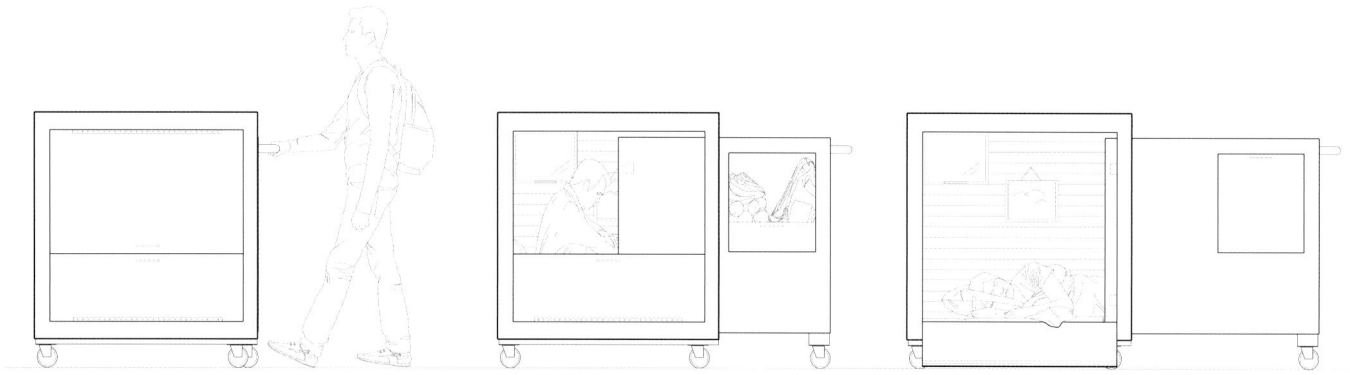

ELEVATIONS

SECTIONS AND FLOOR PLANS

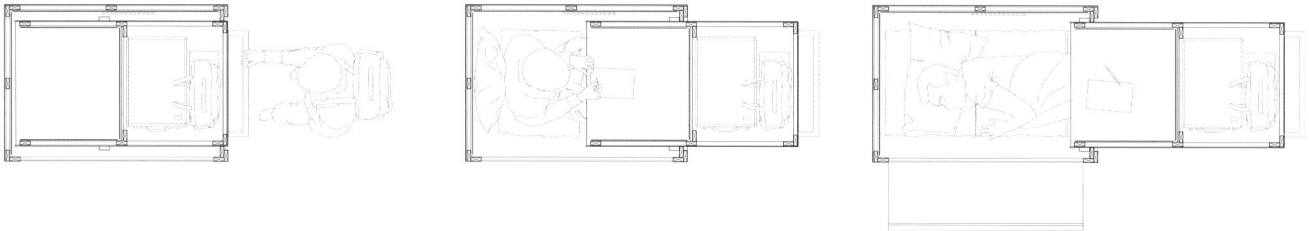

SHOPPING CART SHELTER

Aleksandr Drabovskiy, Ricky Lo & Sohum Bagaria

Shopping Cart Shelter uses the existing system of a shopping cart, an object extensively used among the Los Angeles homeless population, and alters it for the better. The customized shopping cart takes advantage of the possessions that homeless people currently have, which means that they do not have to purchase expensive equipment to enhance their basic standards of living. While a traditional shopping cart can only be used for mobile storage, these design modifications provide several benefits. A portable bed can be taken out of the shopping cart to offer a sleeping experience that elevates a person experiencing homelessness off of the ground. The wooden cover encloses the shopping cart for added security when it is in the compact position. The wooden cover can also be expanded outwards to function as a roof and table for sleeping and dining respectively. Conventional materials such as tarps, ropes, velcro, and zip ties are used for greater privacy and security. The modified system can be mass produced at an inexpensive cost of under $80 USD to fit all shopping cart sizes.

Above: Hadrian Predock, Director of Undergraduate Programs at USC School of Architecture, tests the shelter.

Shopping Cart	1		
Plywood 3/4"	0.5 ~~1.5~~ x $40		~~$60~~ $20
Tarp		$22	$22
Zip Ties		$ 8	$ 8
Hinges	2 ~~3~~ x $ 4		~~$12~~ $ 8
Carabiner	2 x $ 2		$ 4
Lock	2 x $ 3		$ 6
PVC Pipes		$ 4	$ 4
Velcro		$ 4	$ 4

~~$120~~ $76

*Mass produced for < ~~$60~~ $40

THE CONVERTIBLE SYSTEM

COMPACT

PULL

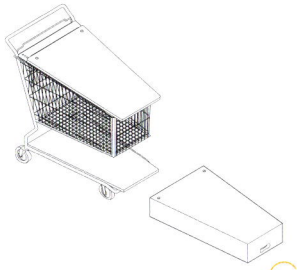

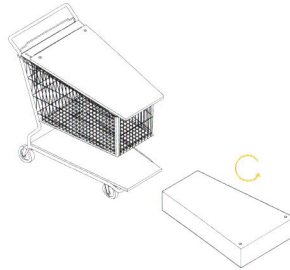

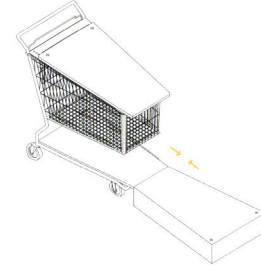

FLIP

ROTATE

POSITION

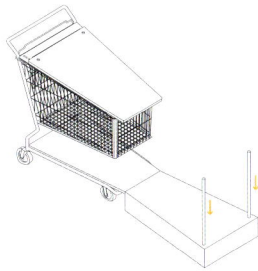

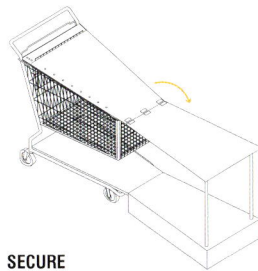

SECURE

ENCLOSURE

NOMADIC NEST

Belinda Pak & Lucy Cheng

The Nomadic Nest is inspired by the bike caravan typology. The use of nested boxes allows for space efficiency for transportation and the luxury of space when expanded. This nesting design also creates a very flexible form, allowing more boxes to attach depending on need. By attaching more boxes, the caravan can accommodate more people and storage with the same simple mechanisms used for the original two boxes. In this design, the larger box serves as the living space. It has space for up to two people, and comfortably fits one. The smaller box is intended for storage. This arrangement allows for the storage to remain immobile and to be accessible while expanded and collapsed.

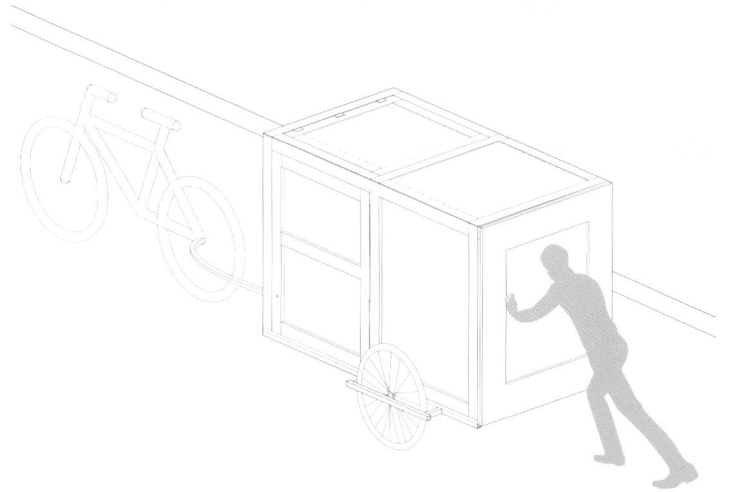

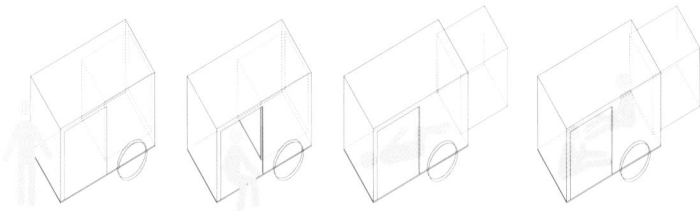

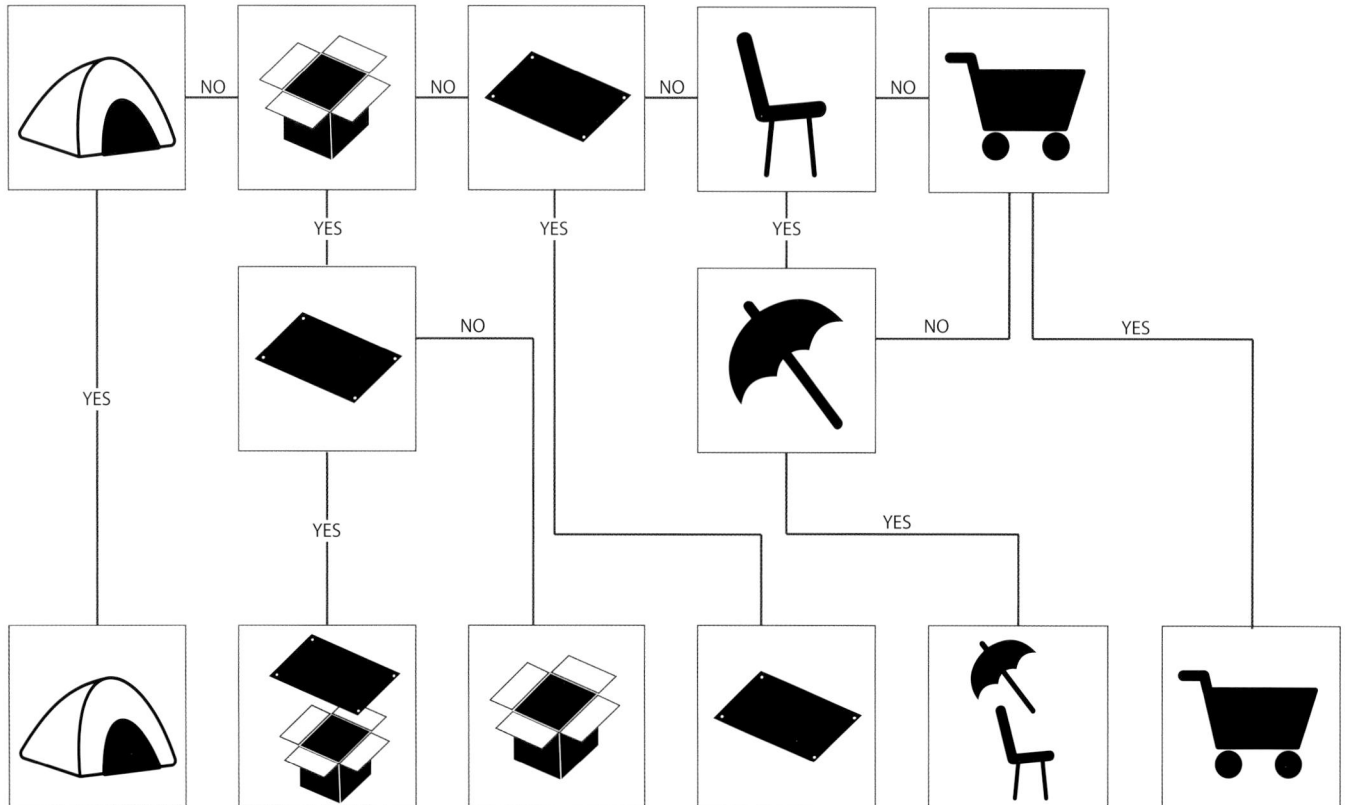

(Photo Credit: John Uniack)

BETTY CHINN

After her family was persecuted by the Chinese government, Betty Chinn spent her childhood homeless and tortured in labor camps. She walked for a year, without shoes, to Hong Kong before reaching asylum in the United States. For the past four decades, Betty has devoted her life to serving the homeless population of Humboldt County in Northern California. Her tireless worth ethic led to her hanging up on President Obama when he called to award her the Presidential Citizen's Medal—the second highest honor in the country—because she "had too much work to do!"

How did you get to Eureka?

BC: I ended up here by marriage. It was an arranged marriage and we moved here the day after the wedding reception. I was living in Seattle before that. My brothers were worried about me leaving. One gave me a rice cooker and one gave me three quarters and said "In case you're in trouble, you can call me." [laughs] And now it's been 45 years.

How did you start working with the homeless?

BC: When I came to this country, I was so grateful for my freedom. When I moved to Eureka, whenever my husband and I would go out to do something, I'd always see someone on the street. I didn't know them but they'd always smile at me. Nobody was upset at me anymore. I didn't see anger in anyone's face towards me anymore. That made me feel good. After a while, I realized that a smile had such a powerful effect on my emotions. I wanted to thank these people for their smiles. But I didn't know where they lived, or who they were. Then I met a little girl who was my son's classmate at his kindergarten. She would sit next to my son when he was eating lunch and look at his lunch pail. So my son would always give her something to eat. Then he'd come home and ask me for more food for the next day. This little girl had no food to eat. After that I talked to the girl's family. It was a mother, father, and two little girls. They lived in a car outside of the Montgomery Ward parking lot. So starting from that point, every night that I'd make dinner, I'd make extra dinner and bring it over to their family. It started with that first family of four and now 32 years later I have more than 500 people to feed.

What was the next step after feeding that first family?

BC: I started to feed more and more people. I started with one spot where I fed people and now I have 12. I fed a lot of people who lived in their cars. I started to meet a lot of veterans. Hearing their stories made me want to help even more. They gave their life for my freedom, but now have ended up in the street. So I take care of all the veterans. I never ask them for anything in exchange for the food. I don't ask them questions. They've been so betrayed. They don't want to go ask for help anymore. After a while, they started to trust me. Some lived in the bushes so I started to go feed them there. This one group lived a mile and a half from the highway. They're the forgotten people. Sixty percent of the people I feed have a mental illness. Economics, drugs, and mental illness, those are the three issues. Doing this for this long, I realize that the more I can touch their lives, the more I can heal myself. Each time when I feed the homeless people, I feel like I'm no longer hungry. Each time I feel for their pain, they take away mine. Feeding them is good, loving them is good, caring for them is good, but after years of doing this I realize that they need to find a way to support themselves. But they have no where to go. That's when I had the idea to open this day center.

Every day we open up. If the people want to change, just bring them over here. Let them experience the world from a different place, out of the bushes, off of the ground. They can come in here, relax, and release their anxiety. If they want help, we can help them. We can contact their family, provide medical help. We have a mobile medical care program. If they're ready to find a job, we help them write their resume and help them find jobs. But even though I'm doing all of this, I do not feel that I'm done yet.

Family is very important to my culture. I see so many broken homes, broken families. The kids cannot go to the shelter. We do not have a shelter for teenagers to stay with their parents. That's such a sensitive age. They need a place where they can rebuild for the future. So I decided to open a family shelter. This shelter can provide support for families with teenagers, little kids, single parents. Before this, they had nowhere to go. This kind of shelter didn't exist before. We're the only one from Ukiah all the way up to the Oregon border. Before this shelter, families would just get separated. I filled the gap. In the women's shelter, only women can stay but the kids can't. Same with the men's shelter. Most fathers have to sleep on the street with their kids if they want to keep their family together. One family I worked with, the kid was born in the car and grew up in that car until they were six or seven years old. Then they came to my shelter. That kid had never slept in a bed before. When I finished this family shelter I felt like I had completed my dream. I felt like I was done. But then two years ago there was this place called Palco Marsh here in Eureka. It was a homeless encampment. The encampment was on city land so the city came to clean it up. There were almost 100 people living out there. I said, "where are they going to go?" I removed 27 families from Palco Marsh. Some I got apartments for and the others we brought to my shipping container village. We bought seven shipping containers and made a transitional housing village. Each container is 40 feet by 10 feet. We divided each container into four units and could take 20 people from the marsh. When they first come in, I let them sleep. I've had people sleep for 20 hours. They tell me they feel safe, that this is the first time in their lives that they've owned a key. That key is such a powerful instrument for them to look for a better life for themselves. Then we help them find a job. Forty-two percent of the people we work with find housing.

When I started that program I had no money and no policy. I had no idea what I was doing. I just wanted to get people in and off the street. I needed insurance, I needed people to cut the doors and windows into the shipping containers. People donated furniture. We just celebrated our first anniversary of the container village. For the first month of operations, I slept in my car outside to make sure they were safe. We have staff, but I didn't trust anyone but myself. I had lawsuit after lawsuit against me for this project. But after one month, the first two people who filed lawsuits came to tell me that they had dropped their lawsuits, that I was doing good work. I'm a very impatient person. I see it, I do it, and if it doesn't work, it doesn't work. I cannot change your life, you have to change your life. But if you're ready to do that, I will 100% stay behind you. Now the city really likes what I'm doing. I document everything. But at the same time, there are so many people against me. Local businesses and organizations accuse me of wrongdoing. So I have to document every single person I help. What time they come in, what time they go out. Luckily the government believes me now, but I still document everything just to be safe. But even now, I don't feel the burden yet. Sometimes I take these things really personally. But then I see young people, like you, caring for the homeless, and that gives me energy again. I still remember President Obama telling me, "Betty, the homeless have no

A look inside Betty Chinn's Container Village, Eureka, CA.

voice. But you do. Speak up for them." So I do. But I also tell all of the homeless people that they need to speak up for themselves. But I'm behind them. I'm their cheerleader. I never give up on people. Just come back when you're ready.

How did you get the city on your side?

BC: I invited the Mayor and all the important city officials to come meet the people we took in from the Palco Marsh. They needed to hear their stories from the people themselves, not just read about it in the newspaper. Seventy-five of us sat down together over lunch and the city patiently listened to the stories of the homeless. That was so powerful for me. They finally spoke up for themselves. They didn't need me to do it anymore. We all have a voice. After that, we partnered with the city and once a year we have a workshop called "Path to Pay Day." We teach them how to apply for a job and invite local businesses with open employment to come interview these people. That's what we're doing today.

"I never give up on people. Just come back when you're ready."

How did you make the leap from feeding people to housing people?

BC: I've been housing people for more than 20 years now. People need homes. Kids need homes. About 20 years ago, I rented a place for one family. The landlord was very good to me and owned a lot of property. For more than 20 years, that same landlord never charged me more than $350 per month. Some people cannot handle living in a house. I come over a lot during the first month and tell them to wash the dishes, pick up their clothes, do the laundry. I teach them how to shop at the grocery store. After six weeks or so, they get used to this way of life. They start taking pride in their space, making their beds. Most people I house end up returning the rent to me in just a few months. They pay me back. I tell them they don't have to pay me back but they want me to use that money for the next people. Some families can't live in a house with a dog. So I had a crazy idea and started buying mobile homes for people. Then they can park in a mobile home park. $325 a month, with a job, they can handle that. That's also what I'm doing right now. We've gotten a lot of RVs for these people. Some have four or five dogs. Who will rent to them? We have a dog obedience school. We tell landlords, "they have a certificate, the dogs are trained." You cannot separate a dog from their owner. That's their family.

What makes your transitional housing projects successful?

BC: My container village is a place to let people begin to detach from the homeless lifestyle. We want them to feel safe but still value things. That's why they still have shared bathrooms and kitchens. Once they're ready, the next step is to move to one of my other shelters, and then a house or apartment. I will call them for the first few months but after that they can call me. I will always worry about them and help. We need to do case management for at least a year to support them. These spaces are about hope. But it's not just about giving hope, it's about these people becoming hopeful and us supporting them through that process.

How do you get your work done in the face of people constantly trying to stop you?

BC: I just keep going. When I ask the city or Obama why they finally are helping me, they tell me it's because I'm the only one who has hung on. Nobody else would do it. I work 22 hours a day. I use my own money. Who would do that? I have no hidden agenda. This is just a way of healing myself and others. Once people realize that, they start to help me. I always am able to do my work for so little compared to what other people ask for.

Homelessness is getting so bad everywhere. What do you think we can do?

BC: Are we going to end homelessness? I don't think so. Not in my lifetime. It's always going to happen. Unless we all do something. Just building little houses for people isn't enough. They can't handle how to live in it without supervision, guidance. Housing is a major problem. It's so expensive. Here in Eureka, we have no rentals. And who would rent to a homeless person? The cheapest studios you can get here are still $700 a month. Plus a deposit. Where do you get the money for that? It's so hard. There are so many people. So many people get stranded up here from all over the world. I sent 478 people home last year. To the Ukraine, Japan, everywhere. Young people. I just sent a nice family back to Los Angeles this morning.

People want to help but it's overwhelming to know where to start. What would you say to those people?

BC: Just try. I had someone who wanted to volunteer for me but they were scared of the homeless. Another person said, "I'll give you $100 Betty, and you solve the problem." I didn't take his money. I said, "You buy what you want with that $100 and pass it out to the people. You need to meet them." That's the only way to get started. You have to know the homeless. It's so easy to just donate and think you've done your part. But you have to see it. If you don't meet the people you don't understand. You'll always be scared.

You experienced homelessness yourself. What elements of that experience have stayed with you?

BC: I was homeless as a child when I was seven years old in China. Not because of the economy but because of a political problem. The three or four years I spent homeless really inspired the passion I have for what I'm doing now. Four years ago, as a grown woman who had lived in America for forty years, I went back on the streets for three weeks. I went to Santa Rosa, Petaluma, and Napa. I spent three weeks in three cities on the streets. I had my phone with me, with that picture of Obama on it [laughs], I had money in my pocket. I carried the same carry-on luggage I had brought to the White House.

Why did you do that?

BC: I was about to open up my center. I wanted to see how I'd feel walking up to a shelter and asking for help. I wanted to see how it would feel to be on the other side of the fence. So I did it. Many of the shelters didn't accept me because I'm Chinese.

In California?

BC: Yes in California! After several days under an underpass I decided I didn't want to be homeless anymore. I decided to go to Starbucks to get a cup of coffee and use the bathroom. But all the employees stared at me and I felt too scared and I left. Being homeless again sucked me into a bubble. I had a phone and didn't even remember how to use it. I couldn't get out. Night after night I slept in the underpasses of Highway 101. When we opened the center, I wanted all the people to be passionate about the homeless. Otherwise don't do this job. You have to have a passion for them, understand them. You need to do your job with kindness. Otherwise this isn't a good fit for you.

> *"It's so easy to just donate and think you've done your part. But you have to see it. If you don't meet the people you don't understand. You'll always be scared."*

What did you learn from those three weeks on the streets?

BC: That experience made me design my center differently. Some people you can't pull out of that world. I couldn't pull myself out. I had everything I needed to get out and I couldn't. After I came home, it took me nine months to go back to functioning normally. I already had a heart for homeless children. But being an adult, that's really hard. Our City Manager told me the other day that anyone who did as much as I do would feel burdened. It's crazy. But I do not feel burdened yet. Once I feel burdened, I'm done. I don't have any plan, I just go with what I see. When I was staying under that underpass there was a woman with me. And she told me, "Betty, we all have hope." I've always remembered that. That's what this work is about.

The communal space at Betty's Container Village.

GREGORY
KLOEHN

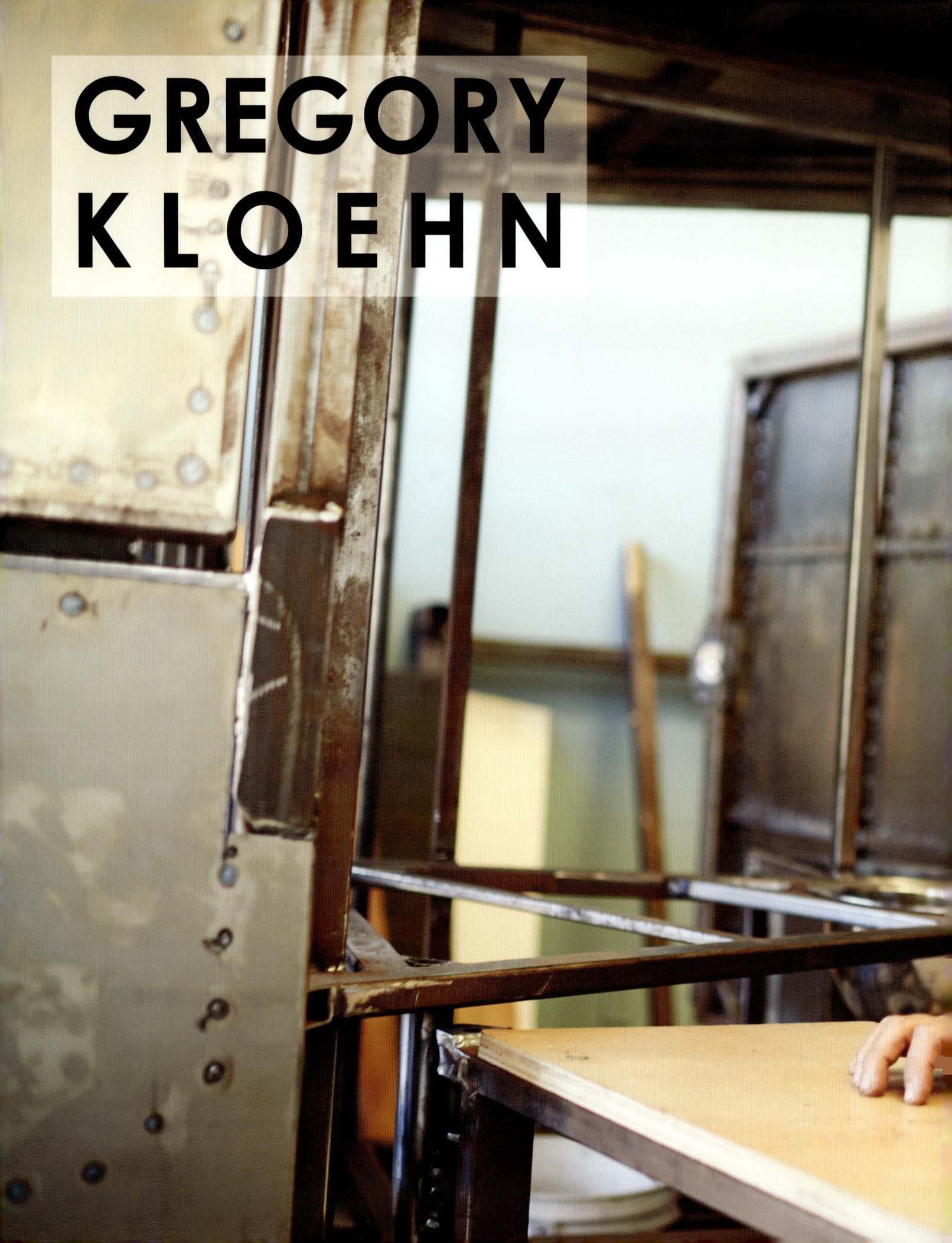

The first picture I ever took on a smart phone was of a shelter created by a homeless person. I had seen so many of these structures around my neighborhood in West Oakland, but I rarely stopped to check them out or see who lived inside. I was always curious but a bit apprehensive and embarrassed to peer into the private space of someone living on the street. When I started looking into homeless shelters, I was struck by how similar their dwellings are to our own. I started to follow the lives of the shelters and the people who built them through photos. As I looked at the pictures I took, I became intrigued by how resourceful and ingenious the homeless are. They take our discarded waste and turn it into the building blocks of their existence. The furniture, pallets, and mattresses we throw away become the components for making a home. The more I documented the homes and lives of the homeless, the more I admired their ability to scratch out a means to survive. I began to see the homeless as a nomadic tribe of the urban jungle.

I became inspired to try my own hand at this nomadic urban architecture. I wanted to make a home from illegally dumped garbage. After a few weeks of collecting materials from the street, I finally made a tiny house out of old pallets, a box spring mattress, a refrigerator door, a doghouse, and a camper shell. I was proud of my home, but didn't know what to do with it. As it sat in my studio collecting dust, it became an impromptu storage space for all my odds and ends.

One cold and rainy night, a local homeless woman named Sheila came by and asked if I had a tarp to keep her dry. I didn't have one and told her sorry. As I walked back into my studio, I passed my little home and thought, "I'll give her this." I ran back out and told her to come back tomorrow and that I would have a home for her. She looked a bit confused but said she would come back. I cleaned out the home and got it ready for the new owners. The next day Sheila and her husband, Oscar, came by my place and I gave them a set of keys and a bottle of champagne and watched as they pushed their new home down the street. It felt so good to give them my little home. They were so happy and I soon realized what a profound effect it had on their lives. They gained the security of having a sturdy shelter and safe place to be. No longer did the rain leak into their bed or the rats run over them while they slept. They now had their own place to call home. I was hooked. I immediately jumped in my van and started scouring the streets for discarded waste that I could transform into more homes.

No matter how or why one becomes homeless, once out on the street these people are subject to the harsh circumstantial conditions that our society imposes on them. Through numerous laws addressing vagrancy and loitering, the very existence of a homeless person can become an illegal act. The people I work with are not the ones who have just lost a job or home and must temporarily live in a car or shelter until things get better. I work with the ones who have lived on the street for so long that a house and job are now foreign concepts, unrelated to the daily needs of their existence.

I never set out to save the homeless, my ideals were not so lofty. I just wanted to make some unique homes and challenge my own view toward materials and their usage. By observing the homeless, I've learned a lot about materials, what constitutes a home, and the human condition itself. So far I've made and given away over sixty-five homes and I'm still making more. It's important to remember that the homeless do have homes. Their namesake describes a limited view of what a home actually is. These structures may not have all the amenities that we deem necessary, but they also don't have the financial and environmental burdens associated with modern homes. These dwellings are more akin to the spontaneous forts one makes as a child from the blankets and furniture at hand, albeit with an impending survivalist slant. The homeless are resilient builders, able to create a shelter on any urban landscape, using whatever they find around them at any time of day. In the end, we all share the same human instinct to find a place to call home.

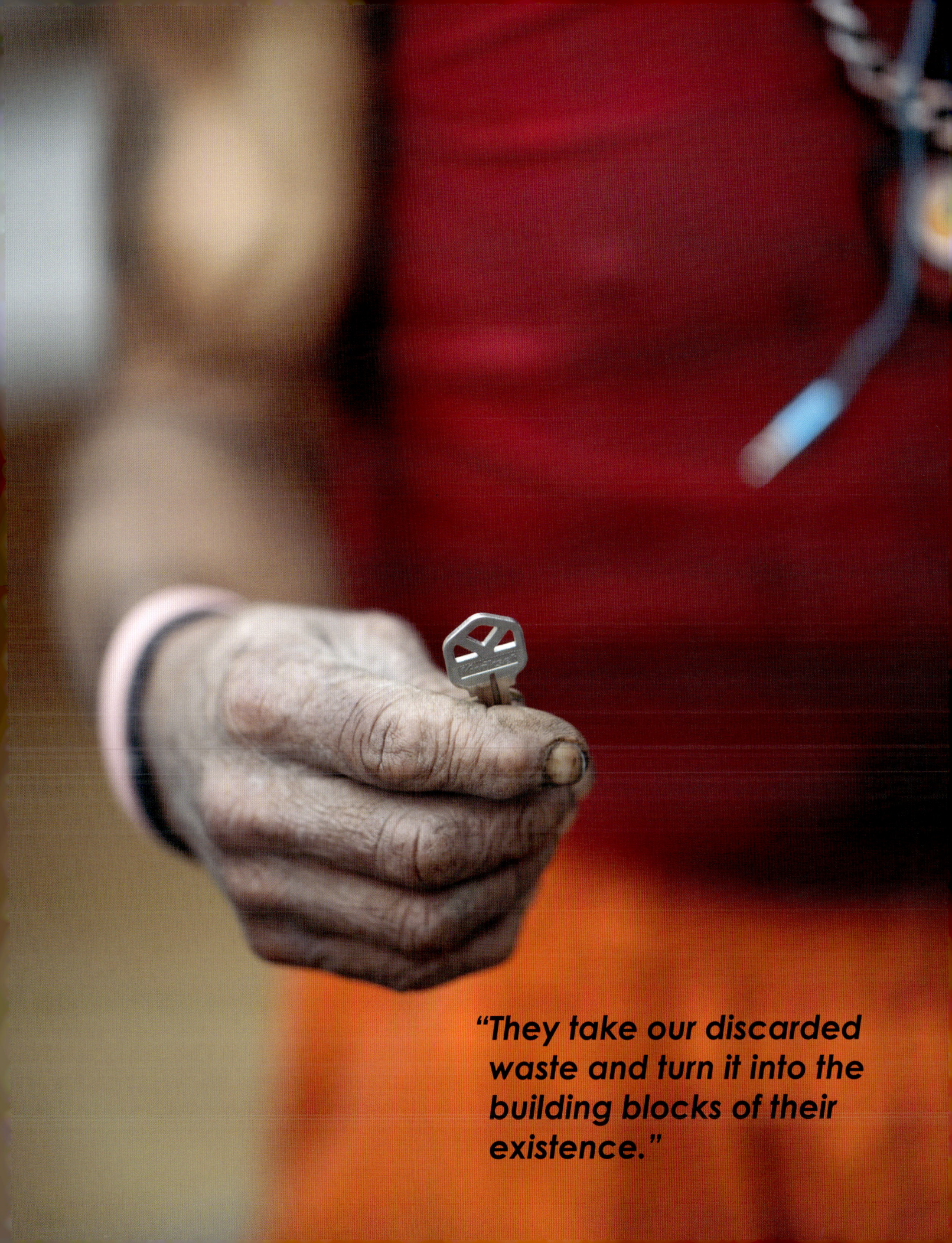

"They take our discarded waste and turn it into the building blocks of their existence."

TINY HOMES WORKSHOP

with Gregory Kloehn

Oakland-based tiny homes builder Gregory Kloehn led a one week workshop with the class following the completion of their nomadic shelters. Students divided into three groups and spent two days scavenging Los Angeles for trash and illegally dumped materials. They then spent the next five days turning trash into treasure in the Watt Courtyard of the USC School of Architecture. While the three projects were allocated a small budget for locks and wheels, everything else was found and repurposed. The three tiny homes would later be donated to an encampment in Vernon, California. The pages that follow document their construction and their life after USC.

BAM

Belinda Pak, Alexxa Solomon & Maria Ceja

BAM House was built from trash largely scavenged from Koreatown. The tiny home repurposes Ikea bed frames, dresser drawers, a refridgerator door, shipping palettes, and more. The home was given to Guillermo, a resident of the Vernon encampment.

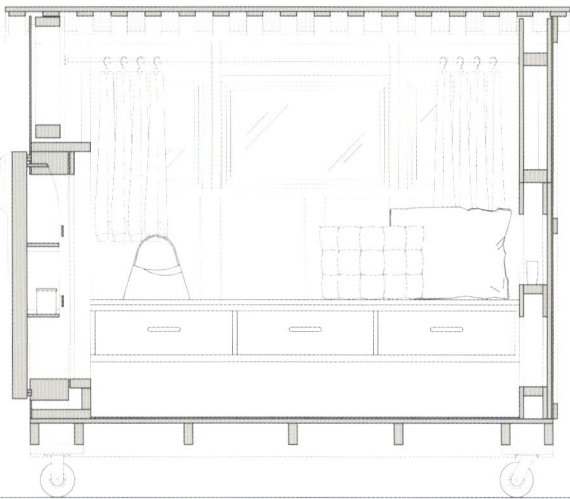
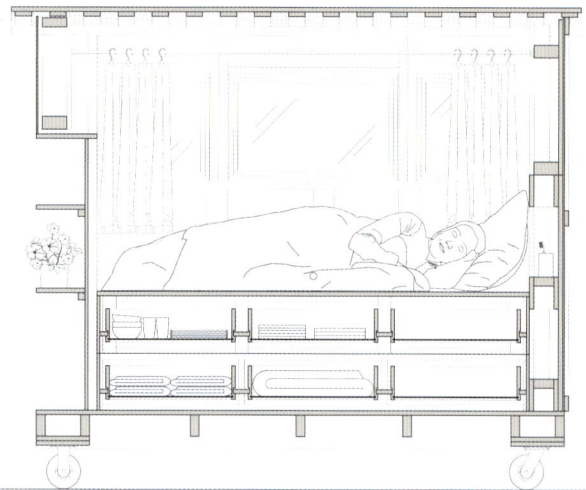

SECTIONS

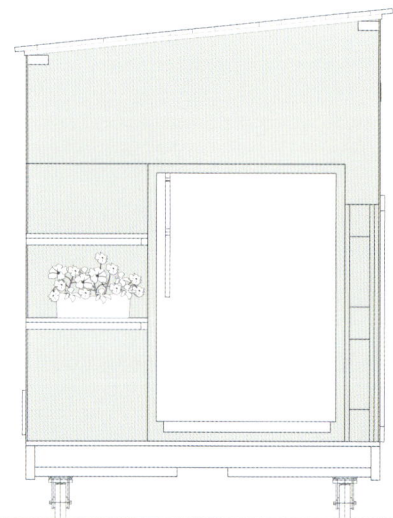

ELEVATIONS

PENTAHOUSE

Jayson Champlain, Joseph Chang, Jeremy Carman & Heeje Yang

The PENTAhouse was crafted from salvaged materials found along the roadsides of Vernon and Boyle Heights, as well as scrap piles near the Los Angeles River and Art's District. From all the found materials, an old truck bed cover had the greatest influence on the design, and lead to the pentagon shape which allowed a small building footprint to provide the maximum living space. The home was given to Marvin, a resident of the Vernon encampment.

ORIGINS	ISOLATION	CHARACTERISTICS	APPLICATION

TRUCK / **BED COVER**

BED COVER
- LIGHTWEIGHT (FIBERGLASS)
- WATERPROOF
- OPERABLE WINDOWS

SHIPPING PALLET / **PALLET**

PALLET
- STRONG (WOOD)
- DURABLE
- READILY AVAILABLE

HOUSE / **HOLLOW-CORE DOOR**

HOLLOW-CORE DOOR
- LIGHTWEIGHT
- EASILY MANIPULATED
- HARDWARE INCLUDED

WATER TANK / **OPAQUE PLASTIC**

OPAQUE PLASTIC
- LIGHT CONTROL
- LIGHTWEIGHT
- SEMI-RIGID STRUCTURE

The PENTAhouse interior staged at USC.

The PENTAhouse interior several weeks after Marvin moved in.

DOUBLE DECKER

Aleksandr Drabovskiy, Ricky Lo, Sohum Bagaria & Lucy Cheng

Double Decker home is made from an assortment of found shipping pallets. The design tackles the relationship between indoor/outdoor and public/private spaces. Maximizing its tiny footprint, the house functions as a private zone for activities like sleeping and studying while the rooftop deck supports gathering and outlook. This home was given to Gio, the brother of Marvin and a resident of the Vernon encampment.

SIDE ELEVATION

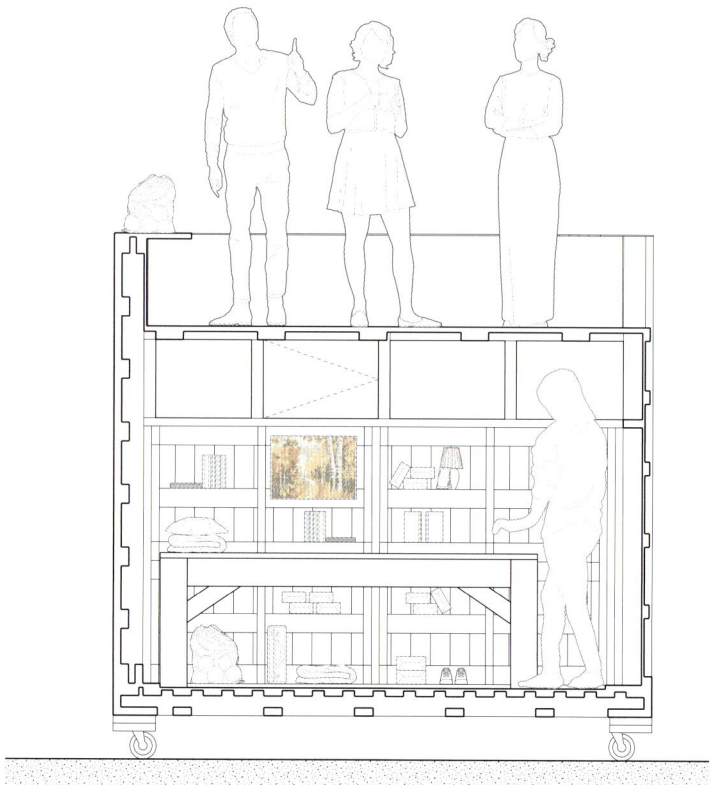

LONG SECTION

A few weeks after the delivery of the tiny homes, the encampment was cleared. Two of the three houses were bulldozed and one changed hands during the commotion. Marvin, Gio, and Guillermo relocated to a new location a mile away near a facility where they could continue to build palettes for income. The following series of images shows the remains of the encampment, the new owners of the surviving home, and the three friends' quest to begin again.

This page: Guillermo gives a tour of his new shelter.

Next pages: Marvin poses in front of the trash heap he cleared by hand; Marvin's new shelter; student Jeremy Carman returns to the new site to donate a bicycle and his nomadic shelter; Marvin, Gio, and Guillermo stand on pallets, ready to build again.

The University of Southern California is a private research institution focused on the public good. We are taking on some of the world's most intractable problems, those that involve multiple disciplines in search of multiple solutions. For homelessness, we are tackling the challenge with social workers, physicians, engineers, educators, and public policy experts. To this list, USC adds architects.

Solving the wicked problems facing the world today. This is our mission, and one that I encourage across the university. Homes for Hope fits that mission.

Cities and counties cannot be expected to "fix" homelessness. Our university, with its expert and inquisitive minds, must be a partner with the community. We are building a multidisciplinary pipeline of faculty, staff, and students who will find state-of-the-art interventions and conduct research that can guide public and private agencies. We can consult and advocate. This is the true model of a university working toward a common goal.

Homes for Hope is exactly the type of project that shows the talent and passion of our faculty and students. These temporary housing units are designed to bridge the gap for those who are between living on the streets and living in permanent housing. They are low cost and portable. It took thoughtful design to develop these prototypes—but it also took deep compassion.

One student who worked on the project said it showed that architecture is not only for those who can afford it. Rather, he said, architecture "can be something that creates social good and changes the way people live their lives." That is exactly the mission of USC, and I am proud to support the work of our architecture faculty members Sofia Borges and R. Scott Mitchell. Their work is a model for all of us.

Michael W. Quick, Provost and Senior Vice President for Academic Affairs
University of Southern California (USC)

MICHAEL MALTZAN

Award winning architect Michael Maltzan began his work on permanent supportive housing in 2003. His ongoing collaboration with the Skid Row Housing Trust includes four projects to date: Rainbow Apartments, New Carver Apartments, Star Apartments, and Crest Apartments. These projects provide 353 homes for formerly homeless individuals, while challenging long-standing stigmas surrounding low income housing. Michael's most recent project with the Trust, Crest Apartments, opened in Van Nuys in June 2017.

How did you get started working in permanent supportive housing and joining forces with the Skid Row Housing Trust?

MM: Rainbow Apartments was the first project I worked on with the Skid Row Housing Trust. The Trust was moving away from a SRO (single room occupancy), hotel, or shelter-like approach. Rather than just trying to get people off the street, they were trying to move that model toward permanent supportive housing. That's how they got involved with us. Permanent supportive housing was a more complex, programmatic approach. It wasn't a huge evolution, but it did mean that the apartments were different, the public spaces and common spaces were different, and all of those pieces added to the complexity of the project.

The Trust knew Inner-City Arts, which was a project I had been involved with for many years that was close to their headquarters. That project represented a type of building approach and level of creativity that was interesting to them. So they first contacted me to look at Rainbow Apartments and we agreed to start working together. And that's really how it started. The Skid Row Housing Trust was trying to reinvent their model. They knew that they needed a different partner and that ended up being us.

Was working on low income housing on your mind before the Rainbow Apartments project?

MM: I had been interested in working on housing for many years but had never had the opportunity to do it. A lot of that had to do with the fact that most of the housing being constructed around Los Angeles at the time was for-profit, developer-based housing, and they weren't very interested in hiring an architect like me. When the Trust approached me, I was incredibly excited because it finally presented an opportunity to do housing. I have believed for a long time that housing is one of the fundamental building blocks for any kind of urban environment, and any kind of innovative approach to the city.

How do you design for people who have spent long periods of time without shelter?

MM: The people who live there are the residents and users of the architecture. But the Trust is the client. And that gives you a two-fold responsibility. One concern is to build a building that serves all the necessary responsibilities that the client has. In the case of the Trust, their priority was to make a place where a community could really develop. It needed to be a supportive environment for the people who lived there at lots of different levels, but also needed to be constructed on a strict budget and schedule.

The other concern was for the residents and their needs, beyond strict programmatic needs. This means looking beyond the square footage, or the bathroom or kitchen. Their needs weren't necessarily different than those of any other person who you would build an apartment for. Residents wanted a place that enriched their lives. They wanted a place that was safe, and had a lot of amenities like natural light and ventilation within their apartments. They wanted a place where they could interact with the larger collective community and still have their private lives. They wanted a place that they were proud to point to and say that they lived there. All of those requirements and responsibilities are fundamentally human ambitions.

In that sense, we try to approach housing projects as we would any other project that we have in the office. We analyze the questions in the same way, we research with the same depth to know what we're meant to achieve, and we try to understand the site, its context, and its sense of place as deeply as possible. The process we engage in is very similar across project types. The process depends significantly on the 3-dimensional digital model and the physical model. There are a lot of investigations and iterations with an eye toward the fact that we are intending to build a building. If I talked about projects like a museum, or a school, or a house for a wealthy individual that I've done, I'd probably say that we went about it in exactly the same way.

What are some of the design features that you carried from one project to the next?

MM: When we did the first project, Rainbow Apartments, it was at a time when the economy was heating up—overheating in fact. The type of contract that the contractor signed was a cost-plus contract, which meant that it included the cost of building materials, with an added percentage for their general conditions on top of it. The problem was, that's an open-ended contract. As the economy took off, construction was getting more expensive. So as we were building, the overall cost of that project was going up. But the budget couldn't change and it meant that we had to continue to pull things out of the design literally on the fly as we were moving forward. It made for a very tough project. A lot of what I believed was the architecture in the beginning ended up being things that we had to pull out of the design. I was almost surprised at how well the building worked in the end for that community.

What I came to realize was that there were still very fundamental architectural ideas, forms, and spaces that were so intrinsic to the design that you couldn't pull them out. Those were things like the large stairs that connected the ground floor to the upper level courtyard. That was a place where people really spent time, met each other, and saw each other on a daily basis. It was a very active social space. The laundry room, as prosaic as it was, became a place where a lot of people connected. Its position in the overall building composition was very important, not only to its success but also how it invigorated the spaces next to it.

The outdoor courtyard space in that building was a little bit blank when we finished it. There wasn't a lot there. But they received some donations and brought in large planter boxes. Those planter boxes became the places that the community grew a lot of the produce that they used in the community kitchen. Something as simple as a garden became an element that the community rallied around. So in that case, we learned something about what the community looks toward to grow relationships.

The single-loaded corridor, as simple of an idea as it is, was hugely important. As opposed to a double-loaded corridor that people disappear into, the single-loaded corridor meant that every time you stepped out of your apartment you were in a semi-public space. That was very important for everybody to have this sense of participating in what was going on in the building.

I started to realize that we needed to approach these design elements in subsequent buildings and projects from Day one. If we could anticipate that those were some of the fundamental building blocks of the building, we would produce something that had a positive

effect for the individual and helped build community. Then we could build on top of that and hopefully create aesthetically stronger buildings. So that first project was maybe the biggest piece of the learning curve in this whole process.

Social hosing used to be know as "The Projects." While some rebranding has occurred since then, a tremendous amount of stigma around the typology of social housing remains. How have you dealt with stigma in your own work?

MM: To a large extent I think it's a question of whether a building feels like it's conveying some kind of institutional quality or not. I wouldn't want to live in a place that felt like it had the imprint of control on top of it. At the same time, I love spaces where it feels like someone has highly considered the design. And those are two very different things. One is approaching design with a very open-minded spirit, a spirit that can accommodate the widest range of lives and lifestyles within the building. It also recognizes that you are designing for a

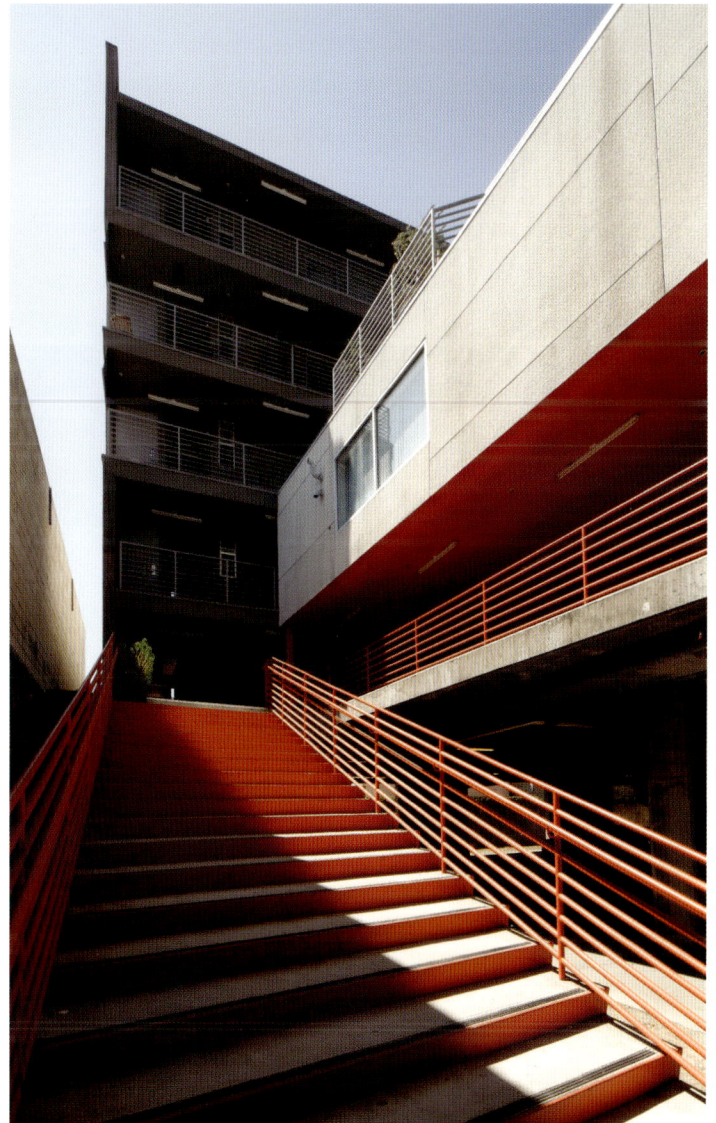

Rainbow Apartments (Photo Credit: Mike Park)

community made up of individuals. How can you provide for individuals without imposing a singular idea of how to live?

If you look at the failure of "The Projects" the grand ideas and the local details both failed. When much of that work started, it wasn't strictly socially motivated or even a response to affordability and the demand for housing, especially if you look at some of the earliest modernist work. The design approach was trying to meet the individual in a very positive, optimistic, and progressive way.

As it continued to evolve, as government became a bigger sponsor for affordable housing, as people felt like they could jump the scale, and as they tried to make it more and more efficient, that sense of the institution took over and it became a kind of lowest common denominator for everyone. They built so much of this type of public housing at one time that it was impossible for communities to take hold in those buildings. It was too much of an instant development. People didn't get a chance to start to make their own lives and communities within them.

There were failures at multiple levels. "The Projects" tended to be motivated by progressive ideals, but were misguided in terms of their ultimate effect. I do consider those lessons learned in the work that we're doing. It doesn't just have to do with the way you build a building; it goes all the way back to where you plan to put the building. The Trust has been very conscious of trying not to build exclusively on Skid Row, but to build in other parts of the city. We make sure the buildings and these communities are more interwoven within the city's fabric and the life of the city around it. We try to keep the building size at a scale that is manageable for a community to develop, and we look for as many opportunities as possible to create more space, and more joy-filled small details in those buildings. It's the thinking at all those different scales that gives you the potential to make something that is a great place to live.

Given our extreme housing shortage here in Los Angeles, what do you see as the optimal solution for re-housing people quickly without reverting back to the mistakes of the past?

MM: Moving quickly can be a positive thing if you're conscious of the history and what likely caused problems in the past. In a city like Los Angeles, it's important to feel comfortable with complexity. Large-scale institutional responses get nervous about this idea. Complexity is important because it's absolutely related to diversity. Having more designers involved produces different approaches and keeps the spirit of experimentation open. It's important to try new things and not

"The city is successful if housing is successful."

be afraid that you might not get it exactly right each time. The wide spectrum of approaches only grows the potential number of options you have as you move forward. That's a very important thing. You shouldn't look for one type of site or try to balkanize or segregate or siloize these communities by building all new housing in one location. We need to engage more creative responses earlier on, before you have a fully realized development project to go forward with.

We've built four projects for the Skid Row Housing Trust now. One Santa Fe also has a portion of it that's affordable, but really it's a market rate, very large project. I've become very interested in the idea of looking for types of building sites in the city that might be possible for this kind of work, and to almost pre-design and begin to experiment with approaches to building on them. These experiments don't rise fully to the level of a typology but their ambition is to create a typological approach to certain site conditions. When you do these exercises on a number of different types of sites, you build up a kit of parts that can give you the opportunity to go into more complex settings and do your work fairly quickly and write in complexity to those typological responses.

The problem of "The Projects" was that they tended to create efficiency by creating a tabula rasa. You'd knock down everything or you'd start with a big open greenfield site where you'd repeat a single model over and over again. That approach is different than trying to anticipate or pre-design more complex approaches to not only housing, but also its impact on urbanism in a city like Los Angeles. Because again, these two things are absolutely and completely intertwined. The city is successful if housing is successful. Housing is successful if it engages with the city in a very real, productive, and positive way.

Do you think that part of what makes your social housing projects so successful in terms of lifting stigma and changing the way people think about this kind of housing has to do with the fact that you don't treat the chronically homeless as different than any other client?

MM: That's absolutely essential. I think architecture has to have a larger cultural and social responsibility. Architecture has the ability to be elastic. What I mean by that is that architecture has the ability to cover many different kinds of projects including affordable housing. But this responsibility should also extend to infrastructure, museums, schools, commercial buildings, and single-family residential projects at the highest economic scale. Architecture should exist in all of those places. If it does, you're inevitably making contributions to the collective urban civic-scape of a city, even if it's one piece at a time. That kind of generous approach to each building block of the city inevitably yields a city that's better for everyone, not only for the people who live in or own a particular building, but for all of us.

This idea that social housing or affordable housing should somehow look like low-cost housing is not only a diminishment to the people who live there, but it's like shooting yourself in the foot as a city. To say that we can segregate our city between the people who have something and the people who don't, or that architecture can't elevate all of those different project types, I find culturally and socially insulting, just as a citizen of the city—forget being an architect. Whenever we've finished one of these projects, we've often been criticized. And I've heard that criticism. People ask, "Why are you building something so nice for that group of people?" My response has always been that we're trying to build something that is nice for everyone. It's terrific that these projects are also a place that people can be proud to live in. But I want to live in a city where all of the architecture is great, is creative, is responsible, is generous, and sees itself as being a part of this larger collective. That's the only way I can image a city can go forward as an inspiring, dynamic place where people want to live.

Rainbow Apartments (Photo Credit: Mike Park)

"I think architecture has to have a larger cultural and social responsibility."

The garden at Star Apartments (Photo Credit: Iwan Baan)

The MADWORKSHOP Homeless Studio partnered with Hope of the Valley Rescue Mission and their CEO Ken Craft for this final project. The assignment called for the development of modular temporary housing solutions to meet Hope of the Valley's growing capacity of residents. These pre-fabricated housing units would act as an intermediary safe zone while residents transition into permanent, supportive housing. Students began by working in three groups to develop three unique, comprehensive proposals. Students then presented their ideas to Ken Craft, Skid Row Housing Trust, and the Department of Building and Safety. Together, the client, city, and local agencies selected a hybrid between the three designs. Students spent the remainder of the semester working as a collective informal office. With a real client and a real problem to solve, students were responsible for working within local building codes and ensuring the modules would pass permitting with the Department of Building and Safety and the Department of City Planning. This final incarnation became the award-winning Homes for Hope.

This page: Shahen Akelyan from the Department of Building and Safety discusses building codes with Ken Craft, R. Scott Mitchell, and Jeff Matt.

Opposite page: Kevin Keller, Deputy Director of City Planning, reviews Homes for Hope designs with students at USC.

HOPE OF THE VALLEY
KEN CRAFT, FOUNDER/CEO

From a young age, whether it was in sports or business, I enjoyed favor and success in my life. In my mid-20's, I started a church that experienced significant growth. Within eight years it grew into a mega-church with thousands attending. While pastoring, I experienced my own personal failure, a failure that cost me everything. I lost my job, my marriage, my house, my self-worth and my self-esteem. Feeling rejected and overwhelmed, I struggled to find redemption. During this dark season of my soul, I was invited to visit a Rescue Mission. There, the Executive Director, who was also a personal friend of mine, walked me around the property introducing me to men who were rebuilding their lives just like me. That visit to the Mission redefined my life. I left the premises that day with a renewed dedication to spend the rest of my life restoring hope and rebuilding lives. I would focus on creating systems and solutions empowering individuals to take control of the future with a renewed sense of passion and purpose.

Born out of my own personal failure, I launched Hope of the Valley Rescue Mission, a place of refuge, restoration and redemption. Hope of the Valley Rescue Mission is a relatively new social service provider within the larger Los Angeles continuum of care. Having started in the summer of 2009, as a hunger relief agency, the organization has continued to grow in influence, services, and programs. Annually, Hope of the Valley now provides over 207,000 meals and 61,000 nights of shelter. In the past 12 months, with the assistance of staff housing navigators and case managers, 128 people were placed into permanent housing. Characteristic of newer non-profits, Hope of the Valley has been able to respond quickly to growing needs and opportunities. Our partnership with the University of Southern California's School of Architecture (USC) was a natural next step in our development. What started as a simple inquiry phone call by professors Sofia Borges and R. Scott Mitchell quickly turned into a joint venture designed to address the rapidly growing problem of homelessness in Los Angeles.

Recently, the Mayor of Los Angeles declared homelessness "a state of emergency" and for good reason. In the past 12 months alone, homelessness increased 35% in the northern part of the city where Hope of the Valley is located. Among the many reasons for the increase in homelessness is the lack of affordable housing. It is not uncommon for homeless clients to possess housing vouchers for six months or more while still living on the streets because they cannot find affordable housing.

This bleak lack of affordable housing brought USC and Hope of the Valley together. We were both searching for a viable solution to turn the tide of rising homelessness. In our first joint session with staff, students, and Hope of the Valley, it became apparent that a traditional model of building affordable housing from the ground up would not be a viable solution to quickly deal with the problem. Traditional methods of securing land, working through entitlements, the Planning Department, Building and Safety, construction, etc. can take between two to three years. With the high cost of land, not to mention the scarcity of it, creating a single source solution of permanent housing through traditional methods was not a viable option. We needed a solution that could be quickly and universally deployed. We needed to launch the Homes for Hope initiative.

Meeting with the USC students on a regular basis turned this initiative from a work project into a passion. The students were focused and determined to create a housing solution that was affordable, practical, functional, and reproducible. After several iterations, and input from the Departments of City Planning and Building and Safety, the students designed and created a modular shelter system zoned as congregate housing, similar to a university dormitory. The beauty of the solution comes from its design. The congregate housing complexes, manufactured off-site, can be installed in as short as two weeks, and if needed, taken down and relocated in the same time period. Each complex would be complete with individual housing units, congregate bathrooms, dining facilities, and social meeting rooms. Additionally, the project would have offices for case managers to ensure clients receive a full array of wrap around services.

What started as an abstract assignment for USC students quickly turned into a problem solving think tank of gifted young minds yearning to create social change through their field of study. The Homes for Hope housing project moved from theory to reality as the students created the first full size prototype, now located at Hope of the Valley's HELP Center in Van Nuys. Currently, the project is awaiting funding to complete architectural and engineering drawings. Once complete, the first congregate housing project will be established. Undoubtedly, once the first site is complete, this creative, affordable solution to housing will quickly be deployed throughout Los Angeles County and beyond.

Thank you Scott and Sofia for thinking beyond mere academia, beyond a "feel good" project. Thank you for believing in the project and the cause behind the creation. You have emerged as leaders and problem solvers on the forefront of a great social problem. Your vision and passion has created hope and a pathway home for the over 58,000 homeless living on the streets of Los Angeles.

I am humbled to be your friend and fellow agent of change.

Photo Credit: John Cizmas

BAM

Belinda Pak, Alexxa Solomon & Maria Ceja

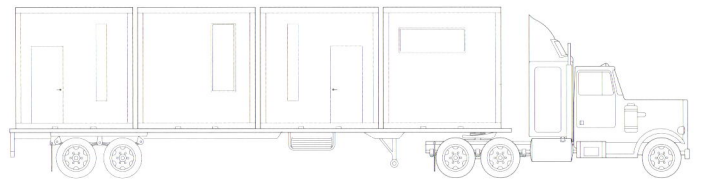

This proposal centers on a modular cube unit, which allows for flexibility in design, ease of assembly, and the ability to aggregate into larger spaces. The module can be flat packed as a kit of parts or prefabricated and delivered to site. The organization of the cubes creates a central courtyard that provides privacy and community space for women who are often victimized on the streets. The lively, open-air environment offers these women a place to heal and restart.

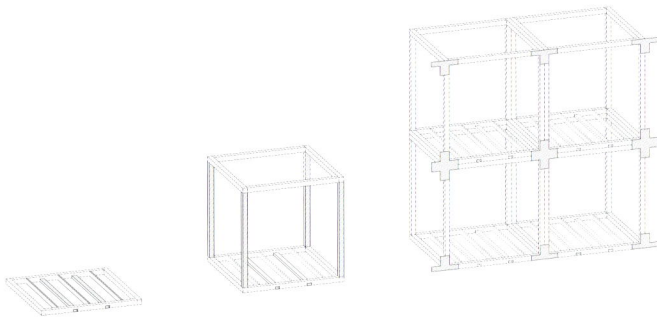

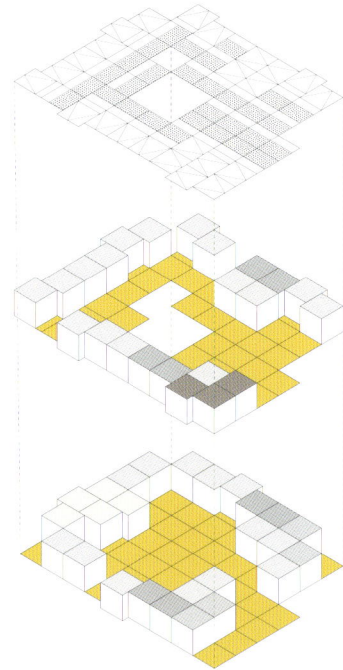

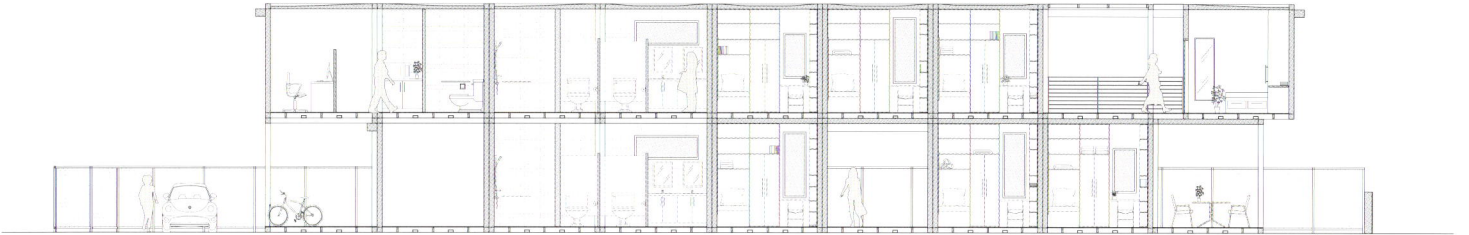

JC3+HY

Jayson Champlain, Joseph Chang, Jeremy Carman & Heeje Yang

This bridge housing proposal focuses on structural and spatial efficiency, reusability, and social rehabilitation. The modular system allows quick implementation onto any flat site by aggregating seismic piers throughout and placing the units onto a pre-fabricated decking system. The units, comprised of steel moment frames and structural insulated panels (SIPs) feature a tilted back wall to maximize the spatial experience inside the unit while giving the exterior a striking visual identity.

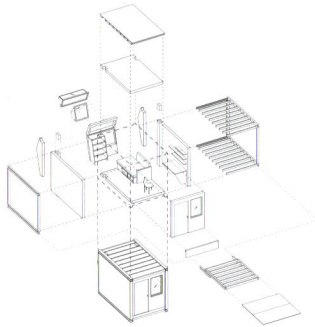

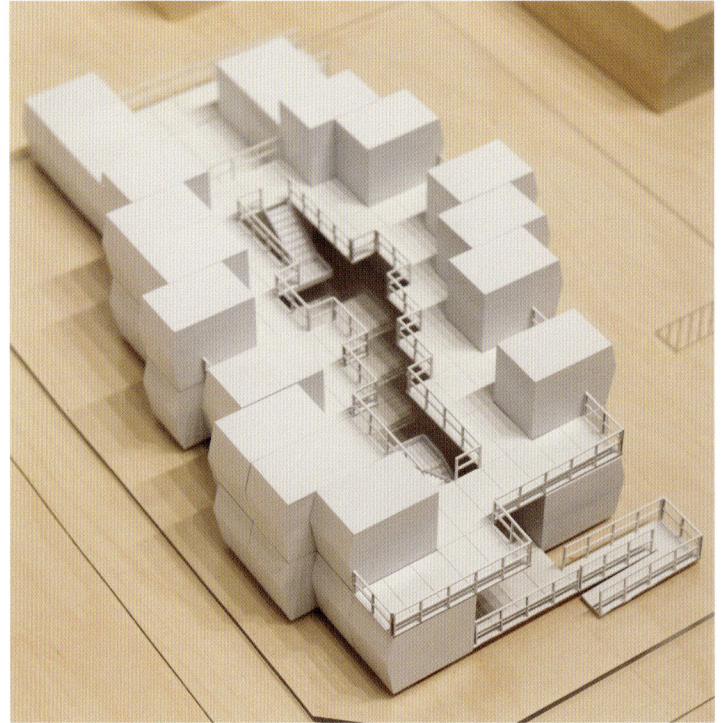

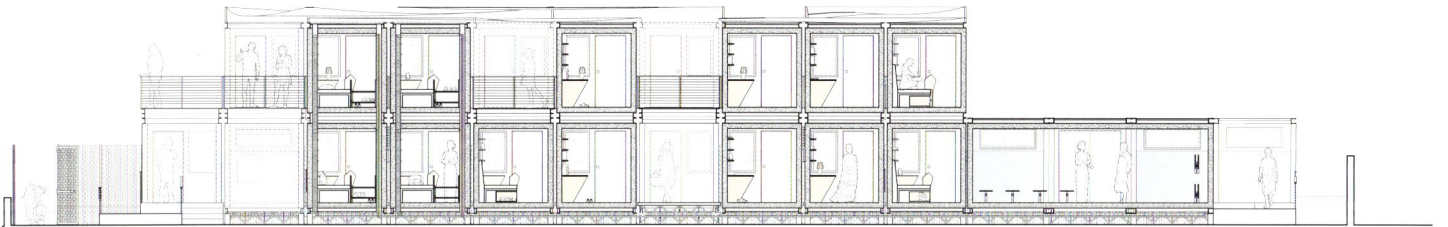

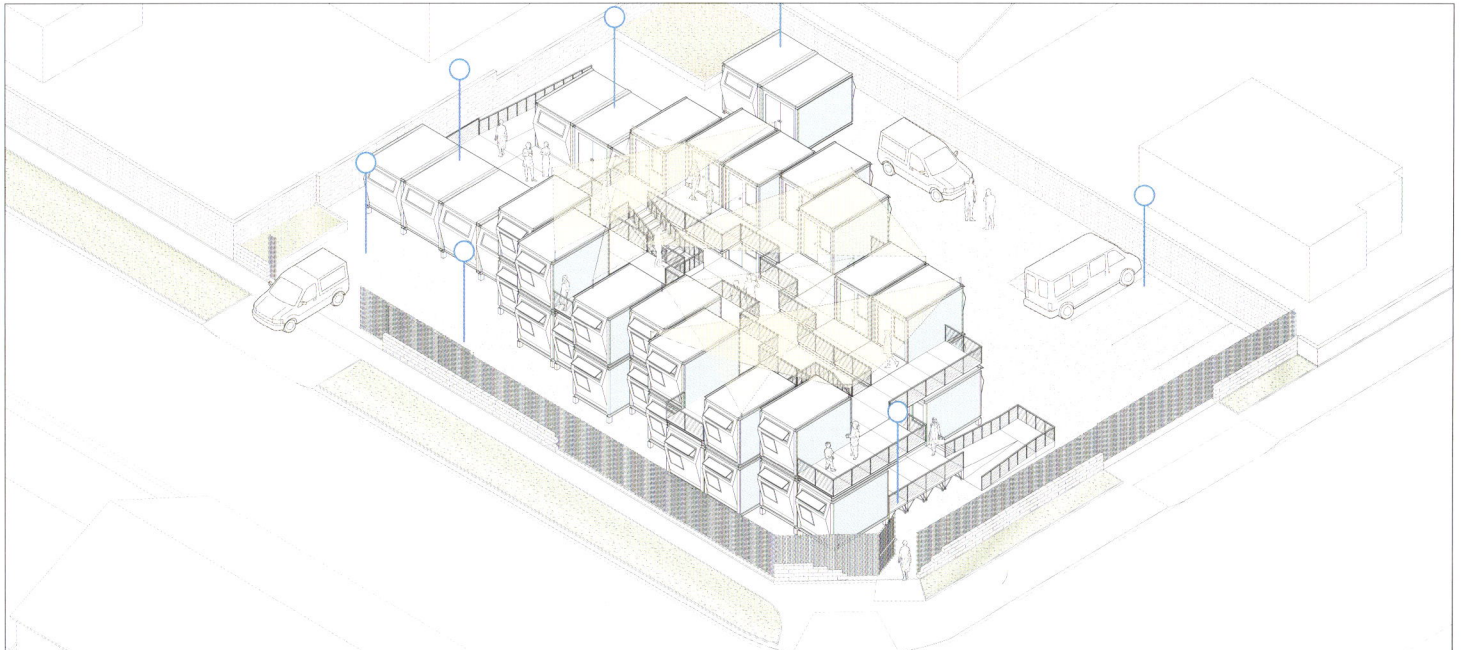

HOMEFRONT

Aleksandr Drabovskiy, Ricky Lo, Sohum Bagaria & Lucy Cheng

Homefront uses two rectangular modules to form the transitional shelter community. The volumes are offset with one another to yield a generous living space of 150 square feet. One of the volumes is then shifted by three feet to create the intimate spaces for sleeping and studying in the two distinct nooks. The aggregated units form a communal courtyard with an overlapping shading system.

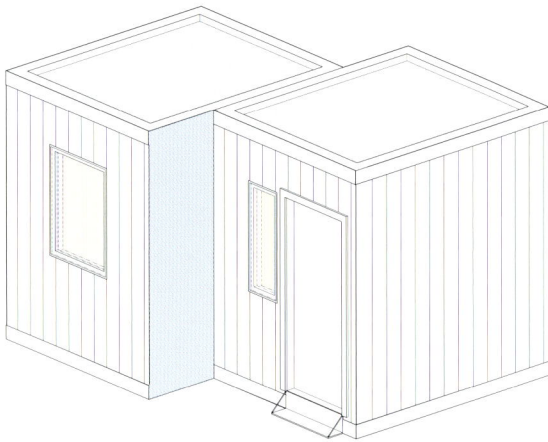

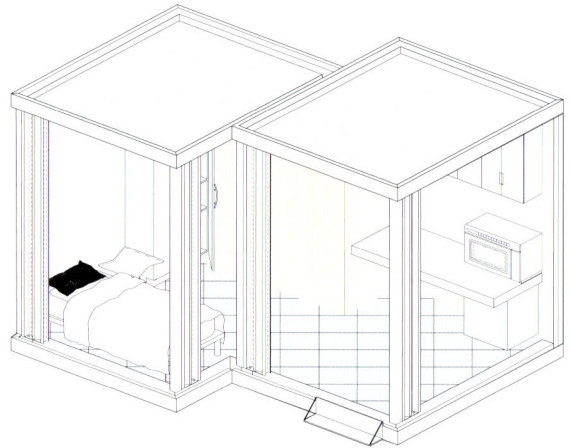

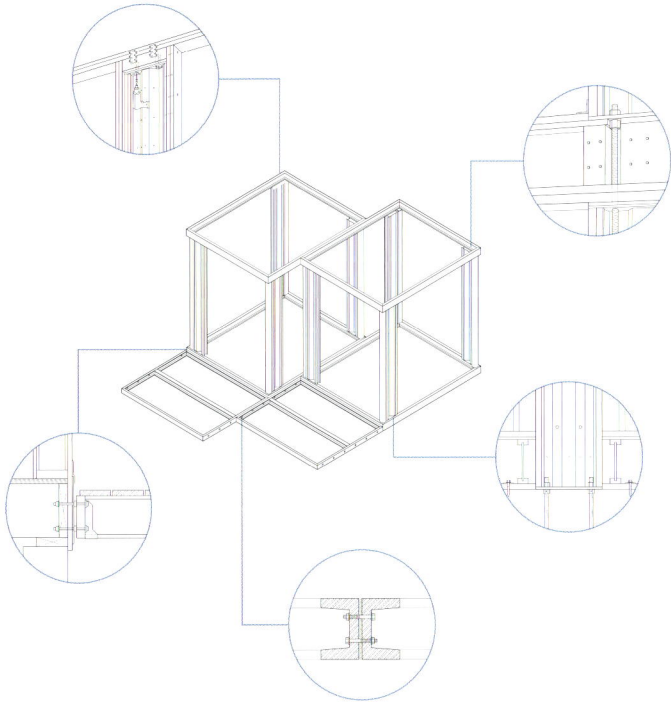

HOMES
FOR
HOPE

HOMES FOR HOPE

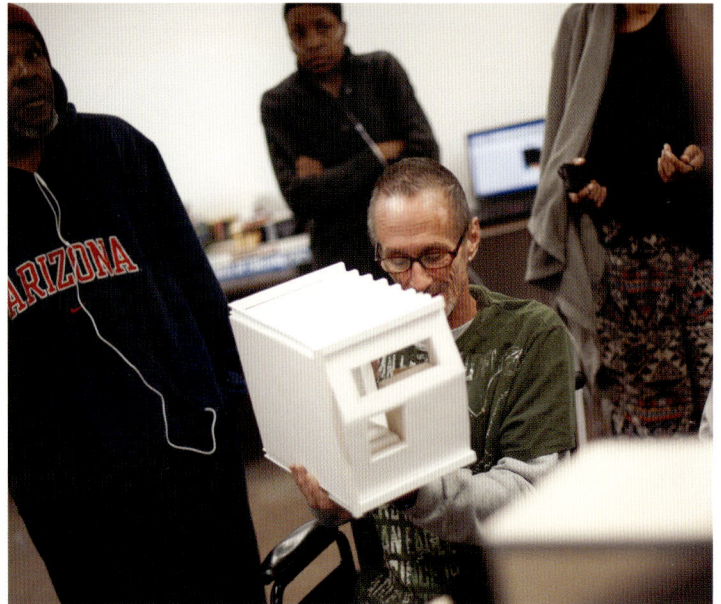

In a city with a vacancy rate of two percent, countless plots of land remain underutilized across Los Angeles. Homes for Hope activates this unused land to provide modular, transitional stabilization housing for immediately sheltering the city's homeless. Installed or dismantled in two weeks or less, Homes for Hope easily reconfigures and adapts to a range of site conditions. The stackable 92 square foot units aggregate into 30-bed communities. The base modules combine to form communal spaces, bathroom facilities, outdoor terraces, and courtyards. Homes for Hope offers an affordable and empowering solution for rapidly rehousing our city's most vulnerable—the first step on one's journey home.

Homes for Hope provides transitional bridge housing to get people off the streets and into permanent supportive housing sooner. While Hope of the Valley is the initial client for this project, the concept of Homes for Hope is not client specific and can be applied rapidly across the city and beyond to meet the growing epidemic of unhoused residents. The Mayor's Office and the Departments of Building and Safety and City Planning became integral allies, optimizing the design and ensuring code compliance. Homes for Hope identifies and works within a number of city zoning loopholes to help people get sheltered faster.

The units aggregating into communities of 30 beds or less, makes Homes for Hope a by-right project zoned as congregate housing. Typical construction in the city of Los Angeles has a lead time of two to five years for every project. This design cuts down on these bureaucratic delays. By developing a pre-approved unit that can be manufactured in bulk quantities, Homes for Hope can be deployed quickly and for a fraction of the price of typical LA construction. The units can be built for $25,000 each, and the price will go down dramatically as more are produced. The stackable living units are all identical, structurally isolated, and maintain their robust integrity as they are reused and relocated from site to site. Each living unit features a warm and bright interior consisting of welcoming amenities that include a CNC-milled bed, dresser, desk, and storage. Units maintain the utmost levels of efficient thermal performance thanks to the use of sustainable strategies like cross-ventilation and passive solar design.

The students built a full-scale functioning prototype of one of the modules by hand in a single week. This module now resides at the Hope of the Valley Day Center in Van Nuys, California. This effort stands as the culminating project of the MADWORKSHOP Homeless Studio. The first pilot project of Homes for Hope will be for senior women in Sylmar, California.

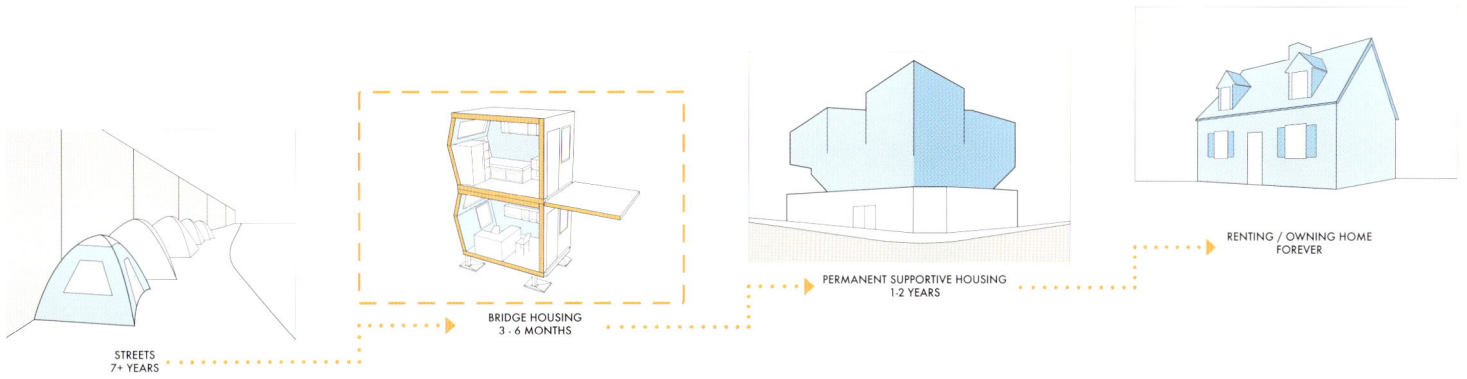

STREETS
7+ YEARS

BRIDGE HOUSING
3 - 6 MONTHS

PERMANENT SUPPORTIVE HOUSING
1-2 YEARS

RENTING / OWNING HOME
FOREVER

Opposite page above: Residents of Hope of the Valley's Recuperative Care Shelter review a model of the residential unit. (Photo Credit: John Cizmas)

Opposite page below: The prototype in transit to Hope of the Valley. (Photo Credit: R. Scott Mitchell)

Following pages clockwise: Frances Anderton discusses the project with students and Ken Craft at Hope of the Valley (Photo Credit: John Cizmas); Deputy Directory Kevin Keller of the Department of City Planning meets with R. Scott Mitchell, Sofia Borges, and David Martin; The class visits the Department of City Planning; Shahen Akelyan of the Deparment of Building and Safety discussing codes with Sofia Borges and Ken Craft.

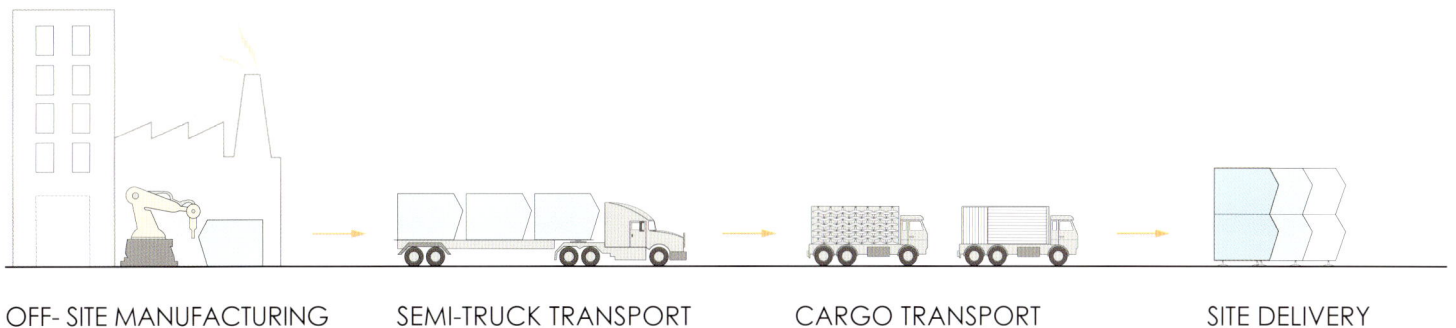

OFF- SITE MANUFACTURING   SEMI-TRUCK TRANSPORT   CARGO TRANSPORT   SITE DELIVERY

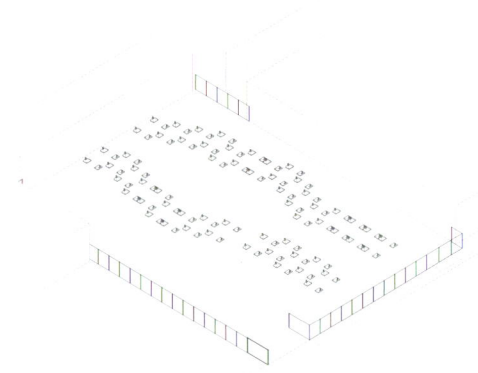

DAY 2 - FOOTINGS

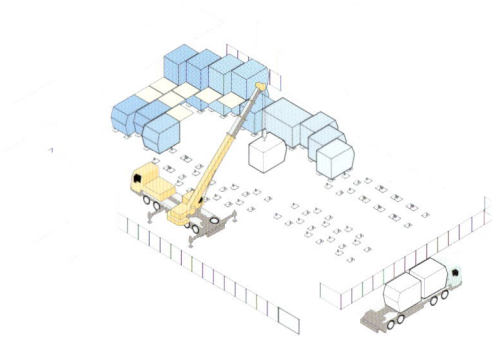

DAY 4 - ASSEMBLY

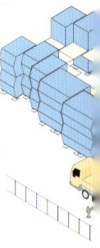

DAY 7 - AGGREGA

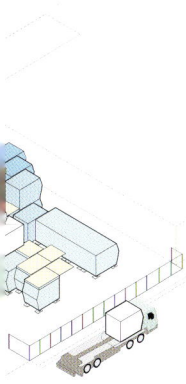

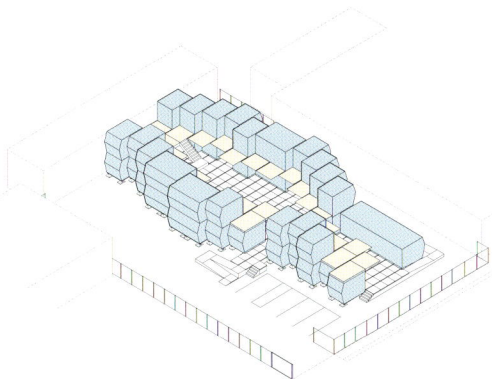

DAY 9 - STAGE

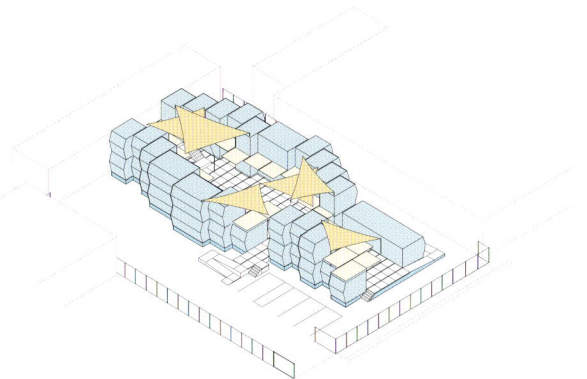

DAY 12 - FINSHING

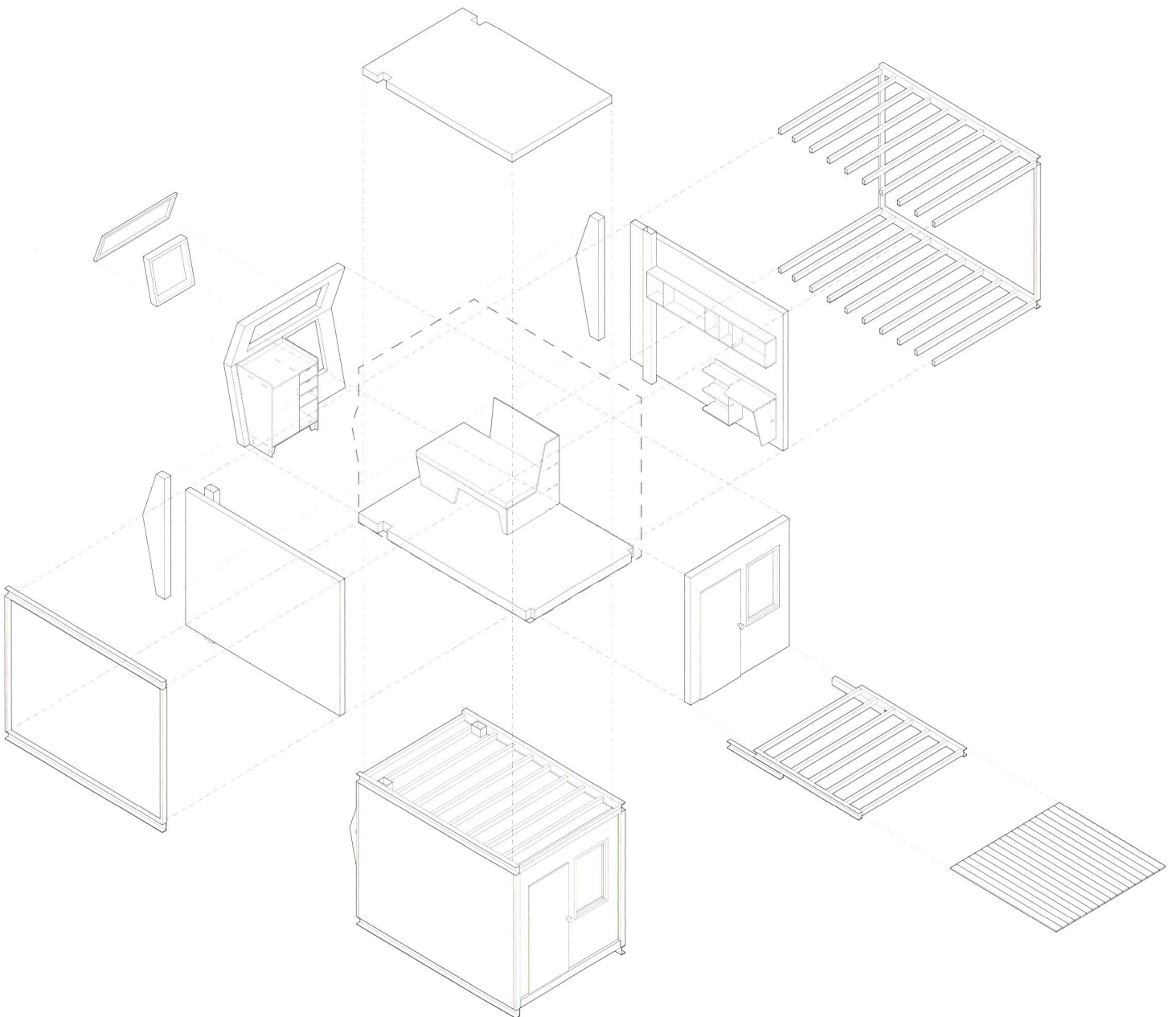

PANEL VARIATIONS

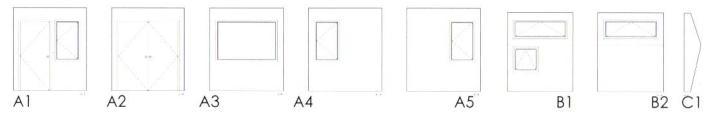

A1 A2 A3 A4 A5 B1 B2 C1

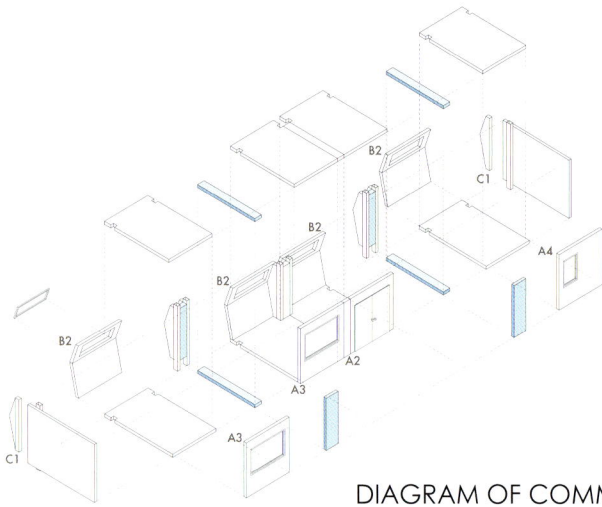

DIAGRAM OF COMMON
AREA COMPONENTS

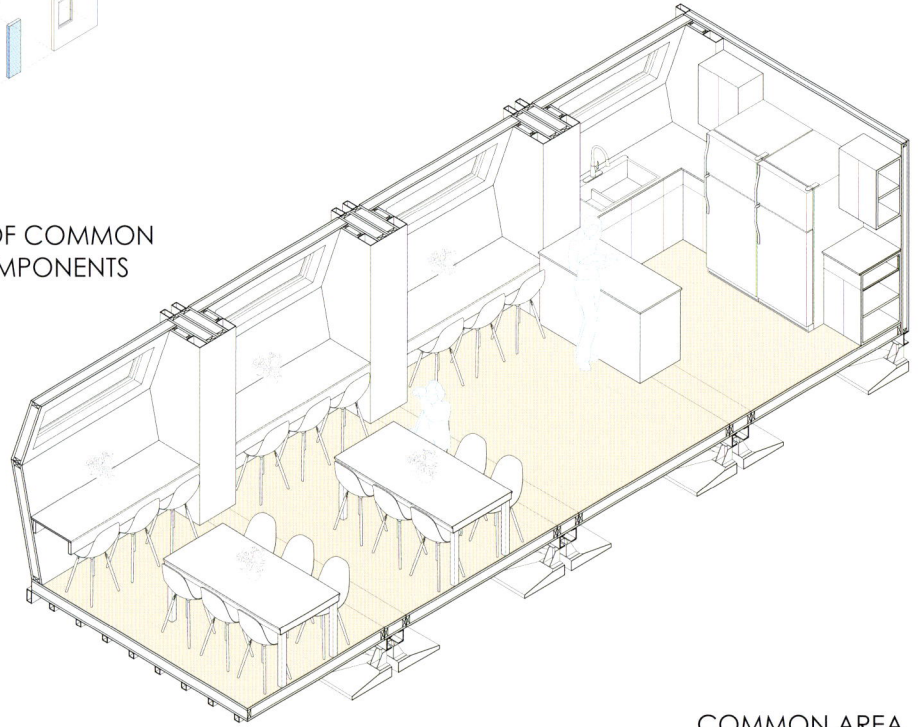

COMMON AREA

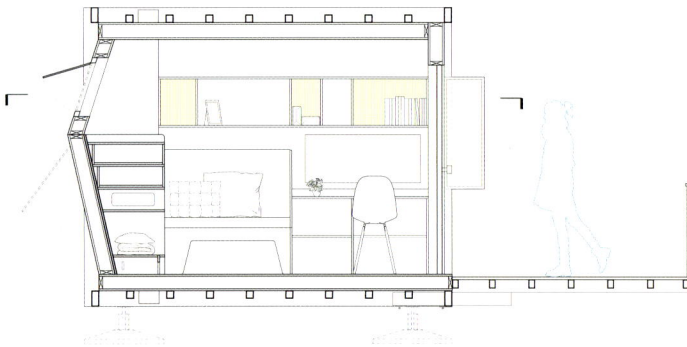

UNIT SECTION

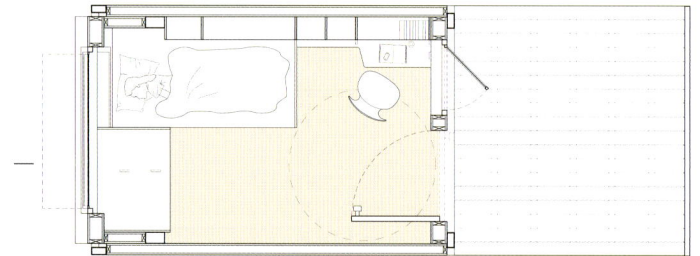

UNIT FLOOR PLAN

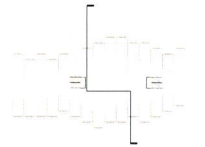

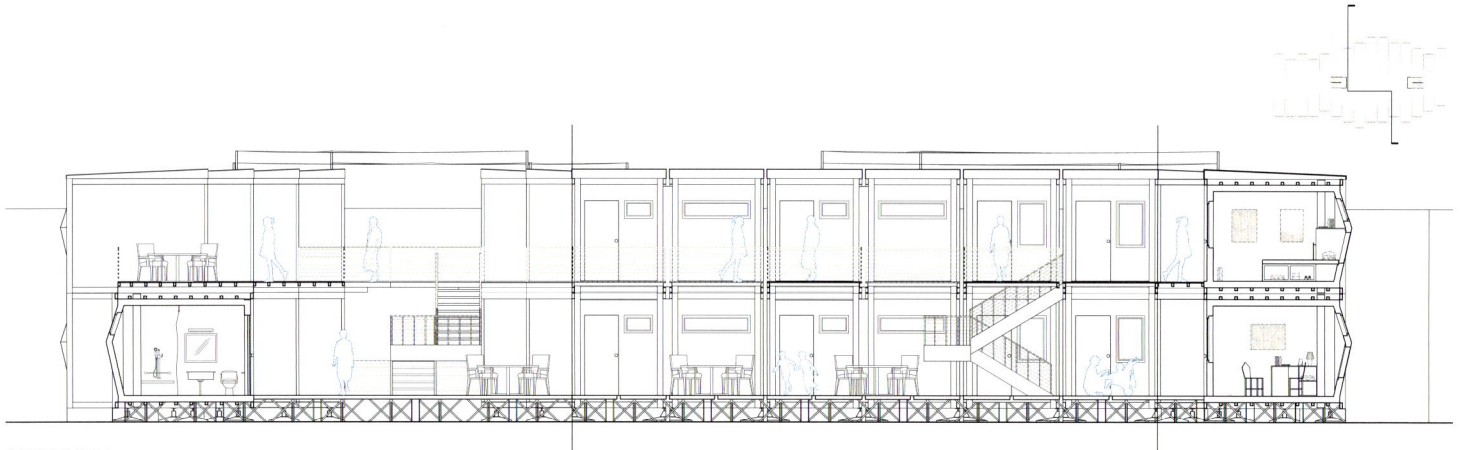

SECTION

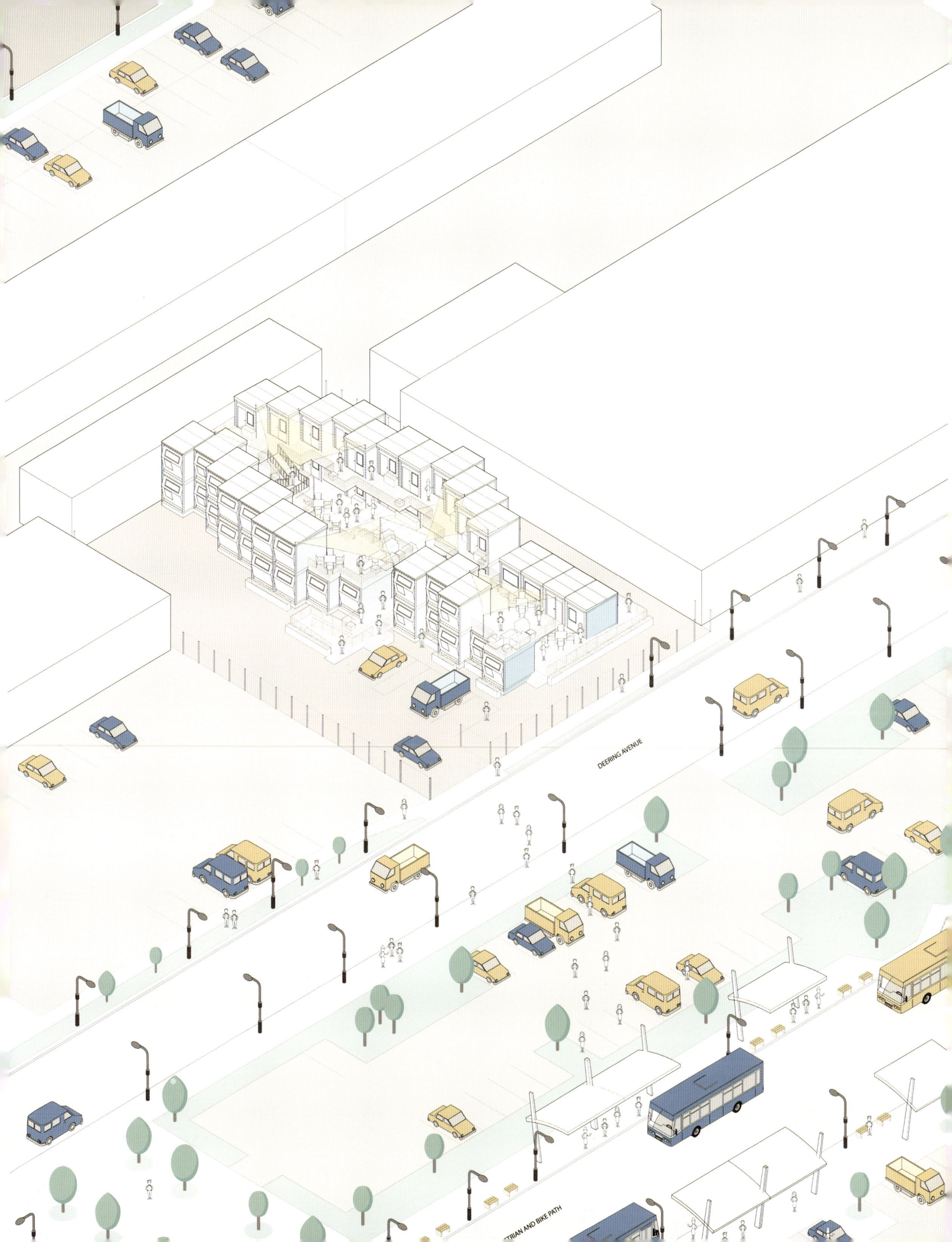

DEERING AVENUE

PEDESTRIAN AND BIKE PATH

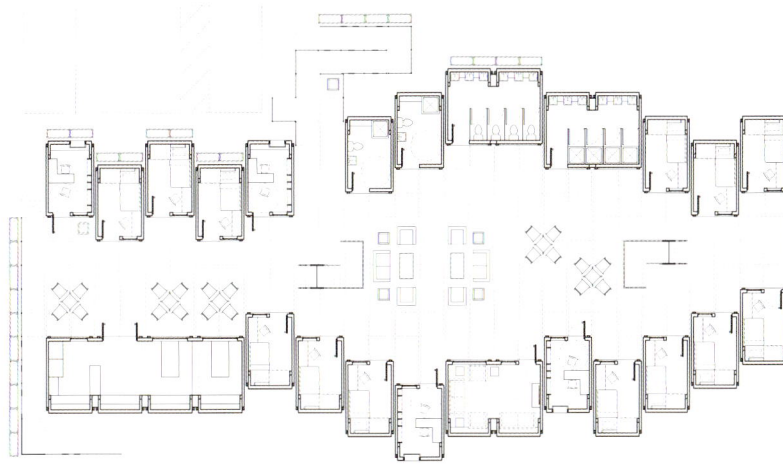

1ST FLOOR PLAN

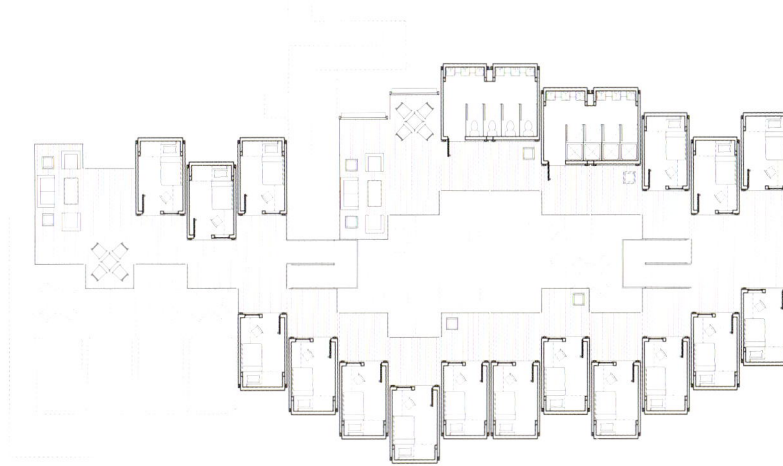

2ND FLOOR PLAN

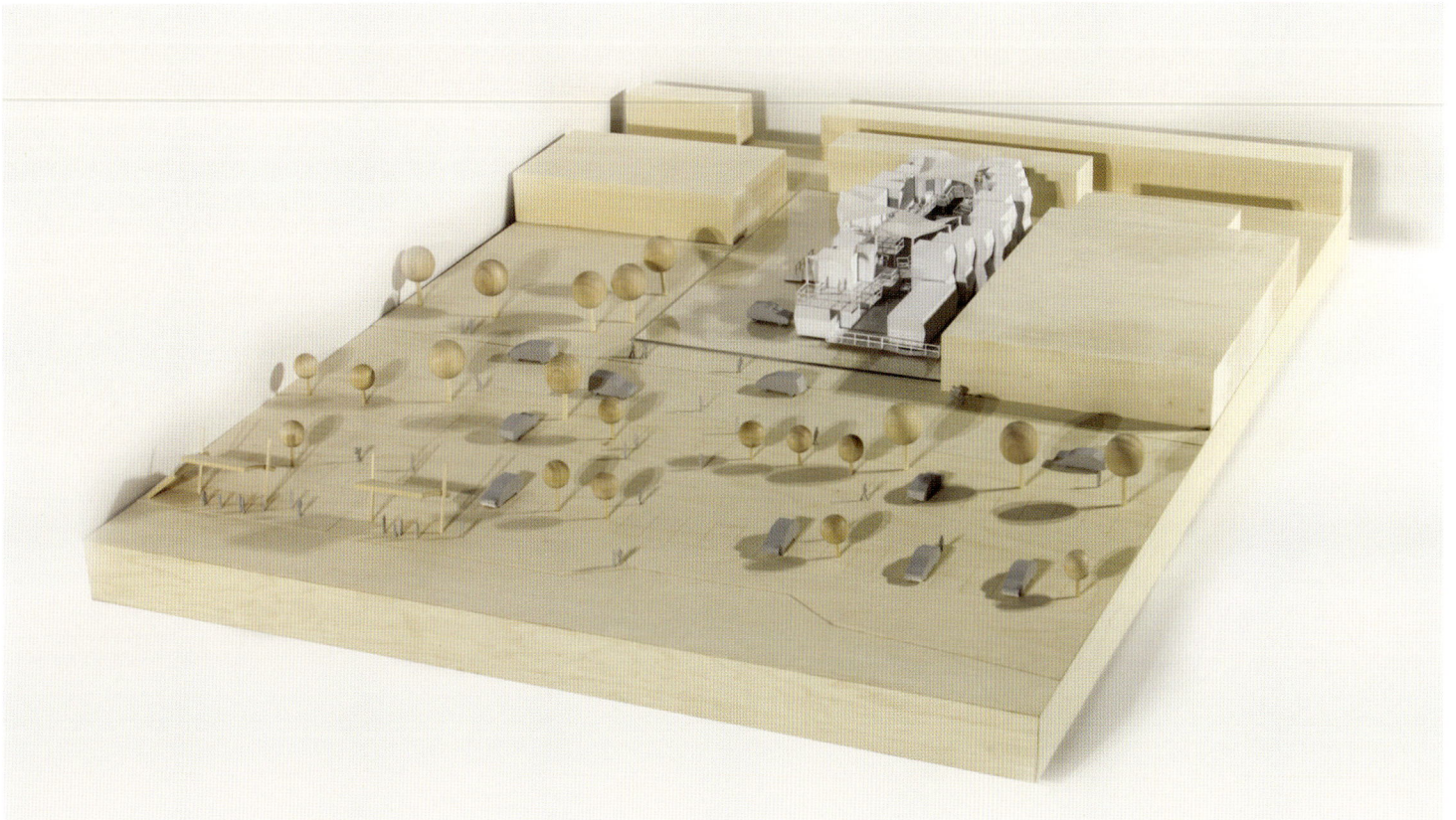

This page: Kevin Keller, Deputy Director of the Los Angeles Department of City Planning and a resident of Hope of the Valley Rescue Mission review Homes for Hope.

Previous pages: The studio visits City Hall and City Planner Matthew Glesne and Planning Assistant Cally Hardy.

(Photo Credit: John Cizmas)

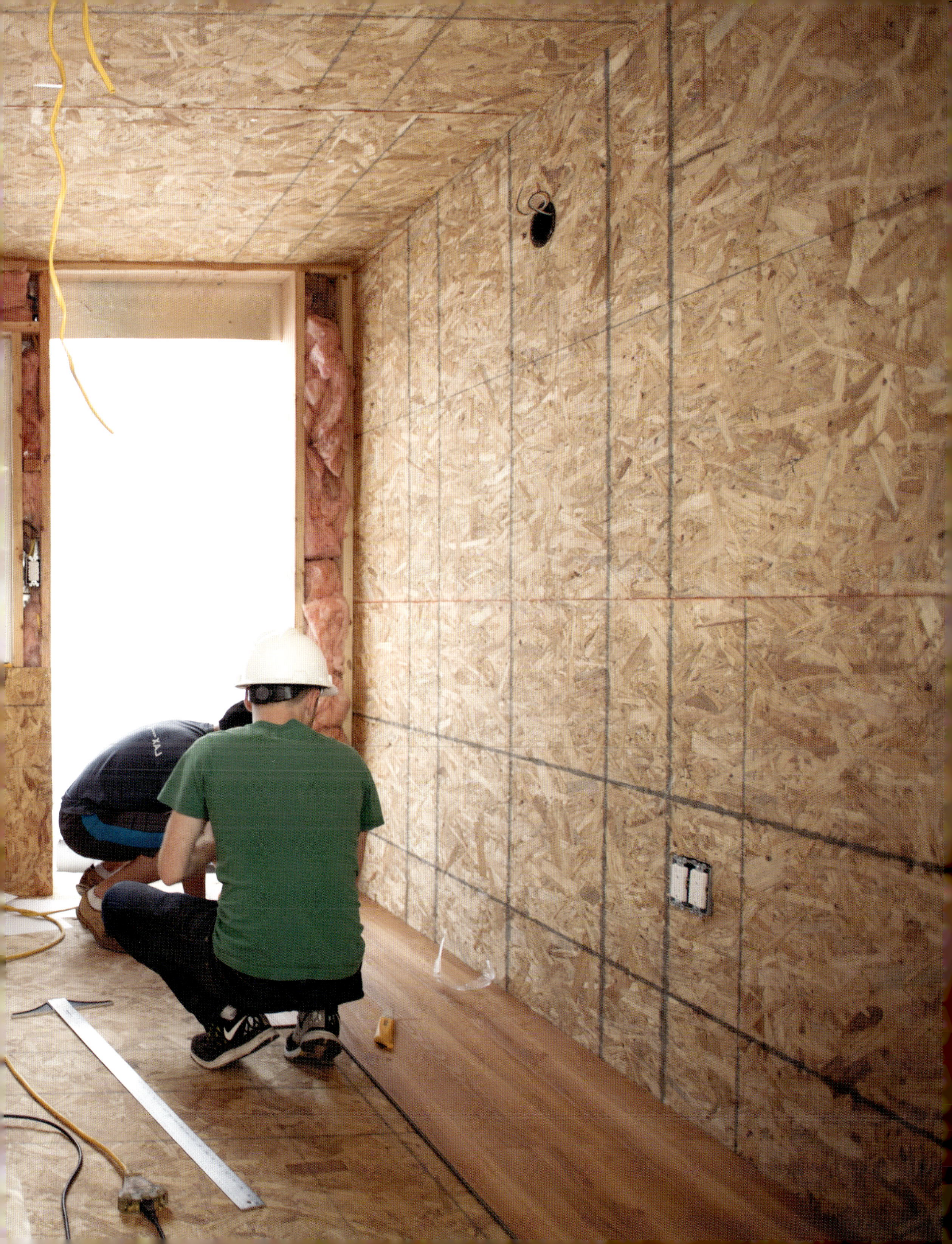

SCHOOL O
GAYLE GARNER ROSK

158492
300-400-1510

Genie
GTH-636

ARCHITECTURE
SCHOOL OF ART AND DESIGN

Above: Rachel Kassenbrock of Downtown Women's Center visits with students and Sofia Borges. Below Arts and Culture Deputy Edgar Garcia explores the prototype.

Following page: Homelessness Policy Director Alisa Orduna and Deputy Mayor of Economic Opportunity Brenda Shockley meet with students and assess the project during final review.

Jayson Champlain

Aleksandr Drabovskiy

Belinda Pak

Heeje Yang

Joseph Chang

Alexxa Solomon

Maria Ceja

Ricky Lo

Jeremy Carman

Publishers of Architecture, Art, and Design
Gordon Goff: Publisher

www.oroeditions.com
info@oroeditions.com

Published by ORO Editions

This book was conceived, edited, and designed by Sofia Borges, R. Scott Mitchell, MADWORKSHOP, and USC School of Architecture

Introduction and text by Sofia Borges
Layout and design by Sofia Borges
Photography by Brandon Friend-Solis
Drawings and renderings by MADWORKSHOP Homeless Studio
Cover photo by Brandon Friend-Solis
Additional photo credits: John Cizmas, John Uniack & Ted Hayes

ORO Project Coordinator: Kirby Anderson

10 9 8 7 6 5 4 3 2 1 First Edition

Library of Congress data available upon request. World Rights: Available

ISBN: 978-1-940743-23-3

Color Separations and Printing: ORO Group Ltd.
Printed in Hong Kong.

International Distribution: www.oroeditions.com/distribution

ORO Editions makes a continuous effort to minimize the overall carbon footprint of its publications. As part of this goal, ORO Editions, in association with Global ReLeaf, arranges to plant trees to replace those used in the manufacturing of the paper produced for its books. Global ReLeaf is an international campaign run by American Forests, one of the world's oldest nonprofit conservation organizations. Global ReLeaf is American Forests' education and action program that helps individuals, organizations, agencies, and corporations improve the local and global environment by planting and caring for trees.